Advanced

Module 3: Word Processing

Matthew Strawbridge

PAYNE-GALLWAY

Published by Payne-Gallway Publishers
Payne-Gallway is an imprint of Harcourt Education,
Halley Court, Jordan Hill, Oxford, OX2 8EJ
Tel: 01865 888070
Fax: 01865 314029
E-mail: orders@payne-gallway.co.uk
Web: www.payne-gallway.co.uk

© Matthew Strawbridge 2006

First published 2006

10 09 08 07 06
10 9 8 7 6 5 4 3 2 1

British Library Cataloguing in Publication Data is
available from the British Library on request.

10-digit ISBN: 1 904467 88 1
13-digit ISBN: 978 1 904467 88 5

Copyright notice

Design and Typesetting by Direction Marketing and
Communications Ltd.

Printed by Printer Trento S.r.l

With thanks to Jim Strawbridge for his help with
testing the exercises.

Ordering Information

You can order from:

Payne-Gallway
FREEPOST (OF1771),
PO Box 381, Oxford OX2 8BR

Tel: 01865 888070
Fax: 01865 314029
E-mail: orders@payne-gallway.co.uk
Web: www.payne-gallway.co.uk

Contents

Preface

Who is this book for?

This book is suitable for anyone studying for **ECDL Advanced Syllabus v1.0 Module 3: Word Processing**, whether at school, in an adult class, or at home. Students are expected to have a level of knowledge of Microsoft Word equivalent to the basic-level ECDL Word Processing module.

The approach

The approach is very much one of 'learning by doing'. Students are guided step by step through creating real documents, with numerous screenshots showing exactly what should appear on the screen at each stage.

Chapter 1 covers topics that are not explicitly in the ECDL syllabus, but which are either important foundation topics or useful productivity tips.

In subsequent chapters, syllabus topics are introduced naturally whenever they are needed in the current document. This helps to demonstrate **why**, as well as **how**, to use these advanced features. Each of these chapters ends with a **Test Yourself** section, which contains exercises that consolidate the skills learned in that chapter.

Software used

For this module you will be using **Microsoft Word**, one of many word processing packages. **Word 2003** has been used in this book, but you should still be able to follow (with a little common sense) if you are using a different version of Word.

Chapter 9 (Embedded Objects) also requires **Microsoft Excel**, since it covers how to embed worksheets and charts created in Excel into a Word document.

Extra resources

The exercises have been designed so that you do not need to load documents from CD or the Internet – you create the documents as you go along.

Useful supporting material, including the documents as they stand at the end of each chapter, can be found on the publisher's website: www.payne-gallway.co.uk/ecdl

1 Basic Concepts

Introduction

This introductory chapter follows a slightly different format from those that follow – there is much more information, and there are fewer practical steps for you to perform.

However, this chapter provides a solid foundation for the more advanced topics. I think you will find that it is well worth the effort you make to carefully read and remember the information presented here. Although you won't be tested directly on most of the tools and techniques in this chapter, a thorough knowledge of them will make you a more productive user of Word.

In this chapter you will

learn what is meant by some of the **terms** referred to throughout this book

learn the use of each of the commands on the basic toolbars: the **Menu** bar, the **Standard** toolbar, and the **Formatting** toolbar

learn about the information displayed on the **status bar**

learn about the **formatting marks** that Word uses as placeholders for non-printing characters such as spaces and line breaks

look at **documents and views**; why you may want multiple views of the same document and how to create them

get a useful list of **keyboard shortcuts**

look at ways of **selecting text** and why you may want to use different methods in particular situations

do some practical work, looking at simple text formatting

learn some **time-saving tips**.

Common terms

Names of keys

This book assumes that you are familiar with the names of the keys on the computer keyboard. Where it is necessary to press a combination of keys to run a particular command, a plus sign is used in the text; for example, you can copy text by pressing **Ctrl+C** (meaning you must hold down the **Ctrl** key while you tap **C**).

Graphical user interface

Figure 1.1 gives the names of some of the **graphical user interface** (**GUI**) elements that will be referred to throughout the rest of this book. It is well worth getting used to calling these things by their correct names, so that you will be able to better communicate with other people when asking for or providing help.

There is an important distinction between the **mouse pointer** (which moves around the screen as you move your mouse) and the **text insertion point** (which is the marker for the location in your document at which any text you type will appear, and is set by clicking the mouse or using the arrow keys on your keyboard).

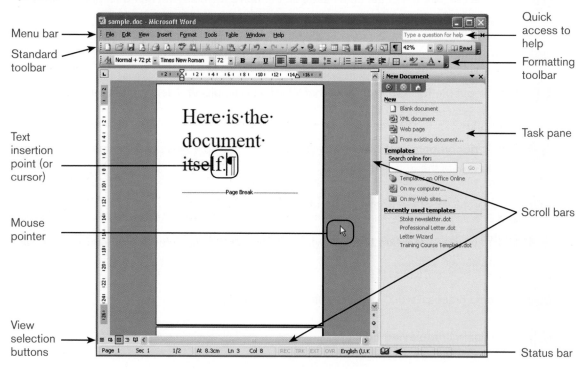

Figure 1.1: Names for parts of Microsoft Word

Toolbars

Menu bar

The **Menu bar** is traditionally docked at the top of the window, although you are free to move it if you wish (this is not recommended). You can undock a toolbar by clicking the drag handle (vertical dots) on the left of the toolbar and dragging it into the main document area.

File   Edit   View   Insert   Format   Tools   Table   Window   Help   Type a question for help

Figure 1.2: Menu bar

By default, Word keeps track of which menu options you use most often and customises the menus to match. Figure 1.3(a) shows a **Tools** menu with options that have not been used recently hidden from view – to get to these, you must click on the down arrows at the bottom of the menu.

These dynamic menus can be useful for beginners, so they don't have to search through lots of commands to find the ones they use frequently. However, as a more advanced user, you might find it simpler to have the menus always expanded. You never need to waste a click expanding the menus, and the positions of the commands don't keep changing. You can set this up as follows:

 Start Word, if you haven't already done so.

 Right-click anywhere in the **Menu bar** then select **Customize**. The **Customize** dialogue appears, as shown in Figure 1.4.

 Click on the **Options** tab to display it, then make sure that **Always show full menus** is ticked.

 While you've got this dialogue open, you will probably find it useful to make sure that **Show Standard and Formatting toolbars on two rows** is also ticked. By default, the **Standard** and **Formatting** toolbars are displayed next to each other with some of their buttons hidden so that both toolbars fit on a single row; setting this option displays both toolbars in full.

 Press **Close** to confirm the change.

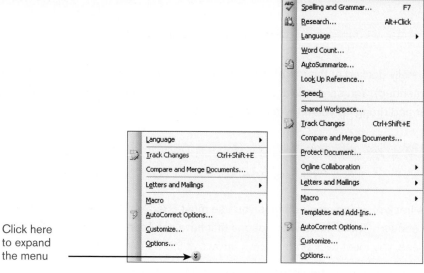

Click here
to expand
the menu

Figure 1.3: Tools menu (a) compressed and (b) expanded

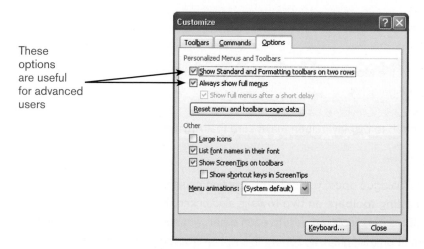

These
options
are useful
for advanced
users

Figure 1.4: Setting options for how menus and toolbars are displayed

Standard toolbar

The **Standard** toolbar contains buttons that provide quick access to the commands that you need to use most often.

Figure 1.5: Standard toolbar

The commands, reading from left to right, are as follows.

 **New Blank Document** quickly opens a new document.

Open lets you browse for a document to open.

Save saves the current document.

Permission is a shortcut to Word's Information Rights Management. You are unlikely to need this.

Print prints the document using default settings.

Print Preview opens a view showing how the document will look when you print it.

Spelling and Grammar finds mistakes in your document and then shows readability statistics.

Research lets you search dictionaries, thesauri, etc.

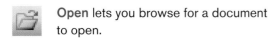 **Cut,** **Copy** and **Paste** let you move or duplicate text.

Format Painter clones text formatting.

Undo lets you correct mistakes.

Redo lets you reapply changes.

Insert Ink Annotations (or press the down arrow for **Insert Ink Comment**) lets you scribble notes with a mouse or other input device. You will only get this button on a tablet PC.

Insert Hyperlink links to another document or web page.

Tables and Borders toggles this toolbar on/off.

Insert Table provides a quick way to insert a table.

Insert Microsoft Excel Worksheet embeds a spreadsheet.

Columns changes the number of columns.

Drawing toggles this toolbar on/off.

Document Map displays/hides the Document Map.

Show/Hide Formatting Marks toggles hidden characters.

Zoom changes the magnification of the document.

Help displays Word's Help task pane.

Shows the current document in Reading Layout.

Formatting toolbar

The **Formatting** toolbar provides quick access to commands that let you change the format of the currently selected text.

Figure 1.6: Formatting toolbar

The commands, reading from left to right, are as follows.

Styles and Formatting toggles this task pane on/off.

Style changes the paragraph or character style.

Font changes the typeface.

Font Size changes the size of the letters.

Bold, Italic and **Underline** make selected text **bold**, *italic* or underlined.

Align Left, Center, Align Right and **Justify** change the horizontal alignment of text.

Line Spacing switches from single to double spacing, etc.

Numbering changes selected text into a numbered list.

Bullets changes selected text into a bulleted list.

Decrease Indent and **Increase Indent** change how far the selected text is indented from the left-hand margin.

Border makes quick changes to the border of text or table cells.

Highlight changes the background colour of text.

Font Color changes the foreground colour of text.

Status bar

This isn't strictly a toolbar (since it is fixed at the bottom of the page). However, you can turn it on and off (**Tools, Options, View, Show: Status Bar**) and it is worth examining the information that it gives you.

Figure 1.7: Status bar

Using the status bar shown in Figure 1.7 as an example, the various things indicated are as follows.

Page 1   the insertion point is in page 1 of the document.

Sec 1   the insertion point is in section 1.

1/2   the insertion point is in page 1, and there are 2 pages in total.

At 8.3cm Ln 3 Col 1   the insertion point is 8.3 cm from the top of the page, and is in line 3, column 1.

REC   shows the status of the macro recorder (greyed = off).

TRK   shows whether changes are being tracked (greyed = no).

EXT   shows whether the extend selection mode is in force (greyed = no). See page 12 for how to use this feature.

OVR   shows whether you are in overtype mode (black) or insert mode (grey, the default). Double-click this to toggle it.

English (U.K.)   shows the language of the text.

The symbol to the right of the language shows the status of the background spelling and grammar checking (in this case, the tick indicates that no mistakes have been found).

Further to the right again is space in which icons appear temporarily to notify you of background saving or printing.

Documents and views

You are probably already aware that there are different ways of showing a document on the screen. For example, there are commands on the **View** menu for switching between five different views of the same document: **Normal**, **Web Layout**, **Print Layout**, **Reading Layout** and **Outline**.

You may not realise that you can display more than one view at once, and that you can split windows to show two different parts of a document in a single window. The following exercise leads you through how to do this.

 Create a new document (click the **New Blank Document** button on the **Standard** toolbar) and type the text **One document, many views**.

 From the menu, select **Window, New Window**. A new window will open, with **Document 1:2** in the title bar (it may be a different number from **1** if you have already created one or more documents since you started Word; the **2** shows that it is the second window open on this document).

 From the menu, select **Window, Arrange All**. Both windows are resized and displayed one above the other.

Although you have two windows open, they are both showing the same information. We can prove this as follows:

 In the bottom window, change the words **many views** to **more than one view**. You should see the change echoed in the other window as you make it.

However, the views themselves are independent, as the following steps demonstrate.

 Click at the end of the text line and press the **Enter** key enough times that the existing text scrolls out of the top of the window. Then type the line **End of the document**.

 In the top window, select **View, Normal**. Use the **Zoom** drop-down on the **Formatting** toolbar to change the magnification to **200%**.

 In the bottom window, select **Window, Split** from the menu. A grey horizontal line will appear, and will follow your mouse. Position the line so that it divides the window roughly in half, and then click. There should now be two independent vertical scroll bars on the right-hand side of the bottom window: use these to scroll the two panes so that the top one shows the first line of text and the bottom one shows the last line of text.

Your screen should now look like Figure 1.8.

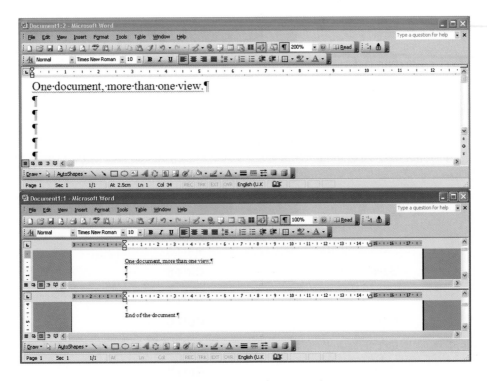

Figure 1.8: Multiple views of the same document

You can use these techniques to help you edit long, complicated documents. Having several views of different parts of the document can save a lot of work when you need to keep cross-referring to information.

Formatting marks

Throughout this book, you will notice that all of the screen shots show the hidden characters. You can toggle the display of these characters on and off using the **Show/Hide** ¶ button on the **Standard** toolbar. I recommend that you keep these marks on display so you can see exactly what is going on in your documents; this way you will get fewer nasty surprises from 'strange' things happening.

Show/Hide

The most common marks are as follows:

Commands

Keyboard commands

It is well worth taking the trouble to learn some of the shortcut keys that Word assigns to its commands. Rather than having to hunt through the toolbars and menus to find a command, it is often quicker to use its keyboard shortcut.

The following list gives some of the most useful shortcut keys; you can find more by searching Word's help.

Command	Keyboard shortcut
Undo	Ctrl+Z
Redo/Repeat	Ctrl+Y
Save	Ctrl+S
Select All	Ctrl+A
Copy	Ctrl+C
Cut	Ctrl+X
Paste	Ctrl+V
Jump to start of document	Ctrl+Home
Jump to end of document	Ctrl+End
Find	Ctrl+F
Go To	Ctrl+G
Bold	Ctrl+B
Italic	Ctrl+I
Underline	Ctrl+U
Lock fields	Ctrl+F11
Unlock fields	Ctrl+Shift+F11
Mark index entry	Alt+Shift+X
Next Window	Ctrl+F6
Normal style	Ctrl+Shift+N
Heading 1 (or 2, or 3)	Ctrl+Alt+1 (or 2, or 3)
Normal view	Ctrl+Alt+N
Outline view	Ctrl+Alt+O
Print Layout view	Ctrl+Alt+P

Selecting text

You often need to format a block of text. Before you can do this, you need to select the text you want to work with. There are several ways to select text. You will find it useful to know them all, so that you can pick the easiest method in any given situation.

 Close the bottom window and maximize the top window, so that you are again working with a single view of your document.

Selecting text with the mouse

 With the mouse pointer over the middle of the word **document** in the first sentence, press and hold down the left mouse button. Move the pointer to the middle of the word **than** and release the button.

Notice how Word has highlighted the whole of the phrase **document, more than** even though you started and finished the selection in the middle of words. This speeds up the selection of complete words (which you often need to do) but is an annoyance if you really were trying to select only parts of words – if you need to do this, you should use the **keyboard** or the **extend selection mode** instead (see below).

There is an even quicker way to select a single word or paragraph, as the following two steps demonstrate.

 Double-click the word **document**. This is the quick way to select a single word.

 Triple-click the word **document**. This is the quick way to select a whole paragraph.

Keyboard

To select text with the keyboard, position the insertion point at the start (or end) of the text you want to select, hold down the **Shift** key and then use the arrow keys to move the insertion point. The text between the original and final positions of the insertion point will be selected.

To move the insertion point a word (instead of a character) at a time, hold down **Ctrl+Shift**. You can use the **PgUp** and **PgDown** keys if you need to select lots of text.

 Try selecting text with the keyboard by holding down **Shift** and moving the insertion point. Try this both with and without the **Ctrl** key.

Extend Selection mode

If you need to select individual characters, or to select text that spans more than one page, then you may find **Extend Selection** mode useful.

 Move your insertion point to between the characters **c** and **u** in the word **document**.

 Double-click the **[EXT]** symbol in the **status bar**. The **[EXT]** changes from grey to black, showing that you are now in **Extend Selection** mode.

 Move the insertion point to between the characters **h** and **a** in the word **than**. Word automatically does the selection for you.

 Double-click **[EXT]** again to leave **Extend Selection** mode.

Simple text formatting

> **Syllabus Ref: AM3.1.1.1**
> Apply text effect options: strikethrough, superscript, subscript, shadow, etc.

The **Formatting** toolbar provides quick access to the most common text formatting commands: **bold**, *italic* and <u>underlined</u>.

However, there are plenty of other options for formatting text, so let's try a few.

 Move the insertion point to the end of the line. Press **Enter** twice to create a gap and a new blank line.

 Type the text **Einstein says E=mc2**.

The **2** needs to be superscript, so we'll use the **Formatting** dialogue.

 Select the number **2**, using any of the methods given earlier.

From the menu, select **Format**, **Font** to display the **Font** dialogue.

 Make sure the **Font** tab is selected. In the **Effects** section, tick the **Superscript** box, as shown in Figure 1.9. Press **OK** to apply the change.

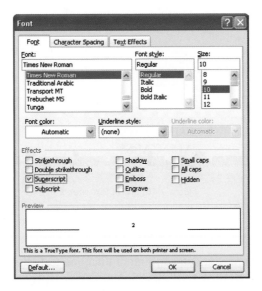

Figure 1.9: Changing the effects applied to text

The **2** is changed to superscript, so that the phrase becomes **Einstein says E=mc^2**. Having seen the principle, let's try out some more of these effects.

 First, let's tidy up. From the menu, choose **Edit**, **Select All**, and then press the **Delete** key. This removes all of the text from the document.

 Change the font size to **18** and type out a list (one per line) of the possible effects that can be applied to text: **Strikethrough**, **Double strikethrough**, **Superscript**, **Subscript**, **Shadow**, **Outline**, **Emboss**, **Engrave**, **Small caps**, **All caps**, and **Hidden**.

 Select each line of the list in turn and use the **Format**, **Font** menu option to apply its corresponding text effect.

Hide ¶

Your document should look like Figure 1.10. Notice the light dotted line beneath the hidden text – this text will not print, and will be hidden from view if you click the **Hide ¶** button (unless you override this default behaviour using **Tools, Options**).

Figure 1.10: List of text effects

Although you don't do so here, you can apply more than one text effect at once, for example to create ~~STRIKETHROUGH, ALL CAPS TEXT~~.

Headers and footers

If you want to include certain information, such as the document's title, on every page, then you can put it in a header or footer. If you need a reminder about how to create headers and footers then follow the steps in this section, otherwise you can skip it (this topic is not on the **ECDL Advanced Word Processing** syllabus).

From the menu, select **View, Header and Footer**.

Make sure you remember this menu option – you can't work with headers or footers without displaying them first!

A dotted line, labelled **Header**, appears at the top of the page, together with a **Header and Footer** toolbar.

Notice that the ruler, shown in Figure 1.11, has two tab stops set: a **centre-align** tab stop and a **right-align** tab stop. This makes it easy to use the tab key to show three pieces of information about your document.

Figure 1.11: A header's ruler, showing centre and right tab stops

Type the text **Microsoft Word** and then press the **Tab** key.

Type the text **Font Effects** and then press the **Tab** key again.

Press the **Insert Page Number** button on the **Header and Footer** toolbar, as shown in Figure 1.12.

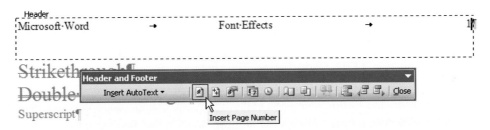

Figure 1.12: Inserting the current page number into the document's header

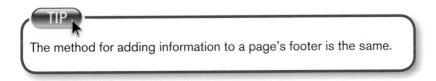
TIP

The method for adding information to a page's footer is the same.

Press the **Close** button on the **Header and Footer** toolbar to close it so that you can once again edit the text on the page.

Time savers

Undo and redo/repeat

To misquote Alexander Pope (1688–1744): To err is human, to **undo**, divine.

We all sometimes make mistakes that cause some unwanted effect in Word, whether it is accidentally pressing the **Delete** key or using some feature of Word that turns out to work differently from how we expected. Thankfully, Word remembers what we have changed and allows us to retrace our steps.

Let's try some ways of accessing the **Undo** and **Redo** commands.

 At the bottom of your document, on a new line, type the text **Did I mean to type this?** If this new text is still hidden (dotted underline), select the line and change the font format to turn the **Hidden** effect off.

 From the menu, select **Edit, Undo Typing**. The line you just typed should disappear.

 From the menu, select **Edit, Redo Typing**. The sentence reappears.

The names of the **Undo** and **Redo** commands in the **Edit** menu change depending on what action each will perform. However, they are always the first two items in the menu and their shortcut keys are always **Ctrl+Z** to **Undo** and **Ctrl+Y** to **Redo**.

 Press **Ctrl+Z**. This is just a quick way of issuing the **Undo** command; the text disappears, as before.

 Press **Ctrl+Y**. This is the shortcut for **Redo**. The sentence reappears.

When you have redone all of the changes, the **Redo** command helpfully changes to **Repeat**. This lets you reapply the last change you made, as many times as you like.

 Double-click the word **mean** to select it. Use **Format, Font** to make the selected text red, bold and shadowed.

 Double-click the word **type**. From the menu, select **Edit, Repeat Font Formatting**.

The word **type** has the same set of formatting changes made to it as you just applied to **mean**. This can save a lot of time if you need to apply the same set of changes to many different parts of a document.

File Search

Unless you are incredibly well organised, you will occasionally forget where you have saved a file. Word has a built-in tool that you can use to track down documents. You will need to know what they are called or some of the information they contain.

There are two ways of file search: **Basic File Search** and **Advanced Search**. When you select **File**, **File Search** from the menu, Word displays whichever search type you used last. You can switch between the two search types using the **see also** links at the bottom of each.

 Save and close the file you have been working on, and then use the **Basic File Search** to find it again by searching for the text **Did I mean to type this** (see Figure 1.13(a)).

 Use the **Advanced File Search** to find all the Word documents that have the word **the** in the file name and are larger than 1000 words (see Figure 1.13(b)). If there are no results, try another search with several criteria.

Figure 1.13: (a) Basic File Search, (b) Advanced File Search

 The **Basic File Search** will find any document that contains all of the words in the search term, whether in the document text or its properties – it does not treat the search term as a phrase.

Document organisation

It is important to remember that the documents you produce have a specific purpose and intended readership. This section discusses some of the ways in which you can use the facilities of your word processor to organise your documents appropriately.

> **Syllabus Ref: AM3.3.1.1**
>
> Understand some important planning and design concepts when considering how to produce information that communicates effectively, by structuring the content to take account of different contexts and audience needs.

You can use your word processor to create many different types of document, from leaflets to mail-merged letters, from posters to books. Before starting to write any type of document, it is useful to plan and design what form it will take. Here are some questions you might ask yourself to ensure that your document communicates effectively:

- Would it be appropriate to add **columns** (pages 51 and 71)?

- Would it be useful to combine portrait and landscape pages? If so, you can do this with **sections** (page 68).

- Could your message be put across more effectively by using **graphics** (page 127) to replace or enhance some of the text?

You must also take account of the needs of your audience. For example, if you were writing a booklet about holidays for the over-60s then you would probably choose to use a large font because some of the target audience may find it difficult to read small print.

> **Syllabus Ref: AM3.3.1.2**
>
> Understand how to produce word processing documents that are complex in terms of content and meaning as well as the understanding, skills and techniques needed to produce them.

Later chapters will introduce you to some of the tools that can be useful when you are managing long, complex documents:

- You can use **master documents** (page 60) to combine many small documents into one large one.

- You can use **bookmarks** and **cross-references** (page 85) to ease navigation around the document.

> **Syllabus Ref: AM3.3.1.3**
>
> Understand how to improve efficiency for users (e.g. use of hyperlinks).

A little effort on your part when producing a document can have a big effect on how useful the document is to your audience. A good example of this is the inclusion of a **table of contents** (page 78) and **index** (page 81) – these elements can make it much easier for people to find the information they are looking for.

Hyperlinks

Another way to improve efficiency, if a document is to be distributed electronically rather than in printed form, is to include hyperlinks. The method for this is as follows:

 Type some text that you wish to have act as a hyperlink, then select it.

 From the menu, select **Insert, Hyperlink** (or press **Ctrl+K**). The **Insert Hyperlink** dialogue box appears, as shown in Figure 1.14.

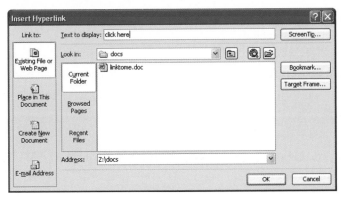

Figure 1.14: Inserting a hyperlink

There are four selections on the left-hand side:

 Existing File or Web Page lets you link to a file on your local disk or network, or a web page on the Internet.

 Place in This Document lets you link to a fixed location in the current document, such as a heading or bookmark.

 Create New Document will create a blank document and create a link to it. This is useful if you wish to create placeholders for information that you can add in later.

 E-mail Address lets you create a 'mailto' hyperlink. For example, you could create a hyperlink that users could click to send you an email with questions or feedback about a document you have written.

 Navigate to the file you wish to link to (or enter the other details, as appropriate) then press **OK**. The text you originally highlighted will now be a working hyperlink.

2 Automatic Changes to Text

Introduction

In this chapter, we will look at some of the advanced formatting options in Word. In order to try these out, you will need to type some text – we are going to use a recipe book as an example.

In this chapter you will

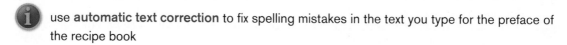

use **automatic text correction** to fix spelling mistakes in the text you type for the preface of the recipe book

write a recipe, using **automatic text formatting** to change the presentation styles for the various elements of the recipe

use **automatic text entry** to save and reuse frequently used text snippets.

Automatic changes

In this section we will look at the automatic text and formatting changes that Word makes on your behalf, how to control what is and isn't changed, and how to add your own customised settings to save yourself time.

There are three categories of automatic changes.

Automatic Text Correction (**AutoCorrect**) finds typos and spelling mistakes as you type, and automatically fixes them for you.

Automatic Text Formatting (**AutoFormat**) takes unformatted text and guesses the formatting that should be applied.

Automatic Text Entry (**AutoText**) allows you to quickly insert frequently used sections of text, tables or graphics into a document.

We will use the example of writing a preface to a recipe book to look at what options are available for automatic changes and how to control them: it can be frustrating when what appears on the screen is not what you type!

Automatic text correction

What is AutoCorrect?

Syllabus Ref: AM3.1.1.3
Use automatic text correction options.

AutoCorrect corrects your spelling as you type. Before trying an example, you need to check that the **AutoCorrect** option is turned on, which you can do as follows.

 From the menu, select **Tools, AutoCorrect Options**.

The following screen will be displayed (make sure the **AutoCorrect** tab is selected).

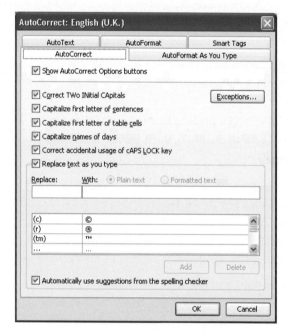

Figure 2.1: AutoCorrect Options

 You'll see on page 24 what these options mean. For now, just make sure that all of the checkboxes (including the bottom one – **Automatically use suggestions from the spelling checker**) are ticked and press **OK**.

It is a good idea to also click on the **AutoFormat As You Type** tab and check that the **Apply as you type: Built-in Heading styles** option is ticked, otherwise the headings in the following exercise will remain unformatted.

You will learn all about **AutoFormat** later in this chapter.

AutoCorrect in action

In the blank document, type the following (exactly as it is shown – the mistakes are deliberate) and watch as Word changes it for you (the deliberate spelling mistakes are underlined here to highlight them, so you don't automatically type the correct word instead!). Non-printing keys you need to press have been given in square brackets.

> **TIP**
>
> The **[Tab]** key is the one with arrows, on the left-hand side of the keyboard.

Preface**[Enter][Enter][Enter]**

[Tab]history**[Enter][Enter]**

This book brings togethr all of the recipes that have been passed down through my famiyl over the past hundred years. it is based upon the handwritten recipe book started by my great aunt Edith in 1880, which has satisfied my family's appetite ever since.**[Enter][Enter]**

[Tab]the recipes**[Enter][Enter]**

There are almots 100 recipes alltogether, ranging from familair favorites to some more modern dishes, orginized by course. Where necessary i have compleatly rewritten the instructions (for example, adding metric measurements), but have tried hard to maintain the traditional style of the original recipe in each case. With the exception of the creme caramel, these dishes are all english, although there are some foriegn influences in the more modern recipes.**[Enter][Enter]**

I hope that you and your friends and family enjoy makeing (and eating) these recipes as much as I have enjoyed cooking them over the years.**[Enter]**

> **Note**
>
> If you **undo** a change made by **AutoCorrect**, Word removes that entry from the list. Therefore, you may find that not all of the underlined words are changed.

Not always helpful

Sometimes you will find that Word is 'correcting' things that are not wrong. When this happens, you can use **undo** to roll back the automatic change (also see the above warning). However, it is far better to understand the available options and to set them up so that real mistakes are corrected, but everything else is preserved.

AutoCorrect options

Show AutoCorrect Options buttons

When this option is set, a context menu offering further options is displayed inside your document for any automatic correction that Word has made (see Figure 2.2).

Correct TWo INitial CApitals

This option corrects the error where you keep the **Shift** key pressed for too long and capitalise the first two letters of a word instead of just the first one. This option only applies to words that are recognised by the spellchecker, so **REal** will be changed to **Real**, but **MYcompany** will be left intact.

Capitalize first letter of sentences

Controls whether Word should fix sentences that don't start with a capital letter, for example changing **this is a sentence. this is another** to **This is a sentence. This is another**. See page 25 for how to control exceptions, such as abbreviations that end with a full stop but don't necessarily mark the end of a sentence.

Capitalize first letter of table cells

This is like the previous option, but applies to text in table cells. If your table cells are likely to have sentence fragments in them, you should disable this option.

Capitalize names of days

Changes **sunday** to **Sunday**, and so on.

Correct accidental usage of cAPS LOCK key

If you have accidentally pressed the **Caps Lock** key then upper and lower case letters will be transposed (since the **Shift** key will make letters lower case). If this option is set and you type **Hello** with the **Caps Lock** on (**i.e. hELLO**), then Word will change it to **Hello** and turn the **Caps Lock** off automatically.

Replace text as you type

This option controls the automatic word replacements that you saw when typing in the preface. A listbox contains the original text and its replacement for each entry (for example, if you type **(c)**, Word will automatically replace it with the © symbol). It is worth familiarising yourself with these replacements, since they will save you time. You will see on page 25 how to customise these replacements.

Automatically use suggestions from the spelling checker

This option will use the spellchecker's dictionary to replace words it does not recognise with a close replacement; for example, if you type **pommegranate** it will automatically be changed to **pomegranate**, even though this is not in the list of replacements.

AutoCorrect exceptions

Sometimes, **AutoCorrect** can make changes that 'break' your carefully written text. For example **3 tbsp. butter** might be changed to **3 tbsp. Butter**. The dot at the end of the tablespoon abbreviation is interpreted as the end of a sentence (so that the next letter should be capitalised).

The simplest way to fix this is shown in Figure 2.2.

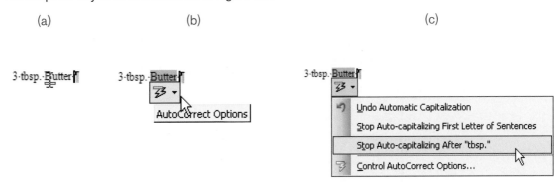

Figure 2.2: AutoCorrect Options button (three stages of display)

Custom replacements

Although **AutoCorrect** is usually used to correct mistakes 'behind the scenes' as you type, you can harness this power to make yourself more productive by adding some custom replacements. You can use custom replacements to set up short references to frequently used, longer terms. For example, if your company is called Great British Widgets, you could add a custom replacement that automatically replaces **GBW** with **Great British Widgets** – three keystrokes instead of 21.

To demonstrate how easy this is, we'll set up a custom replacement so that we can type **choc** instead of **chocolate** in our recipes, and have it expanded automatically.

 From the menu select **Tools, AutoCorrect Options** and enter choc and chocolate as shown in Figure 2.3.

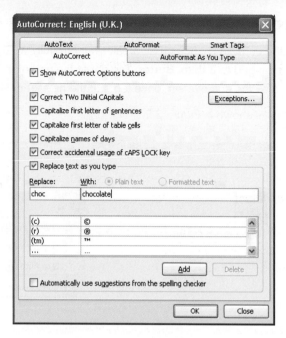

Figure 2.3: AutoCorrect Options

 Press **Add**; **choc** and its replacement **chocolate** appear in the list. Press **OK** to accept the change.

If the **choc** entry already exists (because someone has done this exercise before) then you must press **Delete** before the **Add** button will appear.

 In the document, type the phrase

> Choc sponge pudding

Word should automatically change this to

> Chocolate sponge pudding

You may have noticed a pair of option buttons labelled **Plain text** and **Formatted text** in the **AutoCorrect** dialogue. These were unavailable because we were simply replacing one word with another. However, it is possible to use the **AutoCorrect** options to replace formatting as well as the words themselves.

Suppose we decide to call the recipe book *Great Aunt Edith's Recipes* and want to be able to type the short code **GAER**. When the title is expanded, we want it to appear in italics.

At the very top of your document (above the title **Preface**) type the book's title

---

Great Aunt Edith's Recipes

 With your insertion point in this line, press **Ctrl+Shift+N** to clear any formatting (you don't need to remember this shortcut key, as we haven't discussed **Styles** yet). Click in the left-hand margin to select the new line, and press the **Italic** button on the **Formatting** toolbar.

Italic

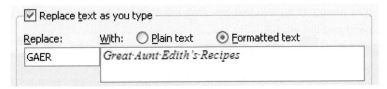 Select the text *Great Aunt Edith's Recipes* (just the text, not the whole line including the paragraph mark) and from the menu select **Tools, AutoCorrect Options**.

 The phrase you had selected is automatically entered in the **With** box. Type **GAER** in the **Replace** box. Make sure that the radio button for **Formatted text** is selected. The **With** text is displayed as italic.

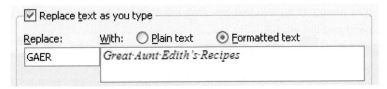

Figure 2.4: Replacing a keyword with some formatted text

 Select **Add** and **OK** to close the dialogue.

TIP

Again, if someone has already run through this exercise, you must press **Delete** before the **Add** button will appear.

 Go to the end of the document and try typing **GAER**. This should be expanded into the whole phrase *Great Aunt Edith's Recipes* in italics.

 Having seen that this works, delete the text *Great Aunt Edith's Recipes* (from both the top and the bottom) and save the document as **Preface.doc**.

Automatic text formatting

> **Syllabus Ref: AM3.1.1.4**
> Apply automatic text formatting options.

The previous step demonstrated one way of changing the formatting of text as you enter it – adding a custom entry that includes formatting to the **AutoCorrect** list.

Word has a more powerful feature, related to **AutoCorrect**, called **AutoFormat**. **AutoFormat** analyses your document (either as you type it, or afterwards, depending on your settings) and makes stylistic changes for you.

To learn how **AutoFormat** works, we'll add the first of our recipes to the book. So that you can see how both the **AutoFormat As You Type** and the **AutoFormat** features work, we are going to go through the following (rather artificial) sequence of steps:

1. Use **AutoFormat As You Type** to make style changes for you automatically as you type the new recipe.

2. Save the new recipe as a plain text file. This will strip out all of the formatting from the recipe, leaving just the words.

3. Open the text file and use Word's **AutoFormat** tool to detect the various elements and apply styles and formats for us.

AutoFormat As You Type

The best way to understand what **AutoFormat As You Type** does is to look at its options dialogue.

 From the menu, select **Tools, AutoCorrect Options**. Click on the **AutoFormat As You Type** tab if it is not already selected, and check that you have the same options selected as those in Figure 2.5.

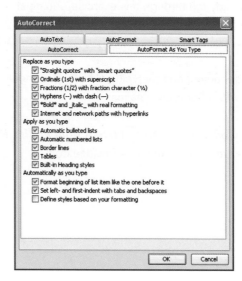

Figure 2.5: AutoFormat As You Type options

Replacing hyphens with dashes
En dashes are used for number ranges (e.g. 3–10) and the longer em dashes can be used for separating clauses in a sentence — such as this one. If there is a space before the hyphens, they will be converted to an en dash (**3 --10** becomes **3 –10**); if there are two hyphens with no space before them they will be converted to an em dash (**Everest--top of the world** becomes **Everest—top of the world**).

Automatic bulleted lists
If you start a line with a 'bullet' character (an asterisk, one hyphen, two hyphens, a greater-than sign, or an 'arrow' (-> or =>)) followed by a space or a tab then, when you press **Enter** at the end of the line, Word will start a bulleted list using bullet characters ●, –, ■, ➢, ➔, or ⇨ respectively.

Try an example using **AutoFormat As You Type**.

 Close **Preface.doc** by selecting **File**, **Close** from the menu.

 In a **new** document, type the text below exactly as it is given. Non-printing keys you need to press have been given in square brackets. Pay attention to how Word changes the formatting as you type.

Stuffed Courgettes[Enter][Enter][Enter]
[Tab]Ingredients[Enter][Enter][Enter]
[Tab][Tab]For the stuffing[Enter][Enter]
*[Tab]1/4 kg minced beef[Enter]
28g butter[Enter]
1 cup of rice[Enter]
1 chicken stock cube[Enter]
4 tbsp. mixed spice[Enter]
Salt and *sugar* to taste[Enter][Enter]
[Space][Tab][Tab]For the sauce[Enter][Enter]
*[Tab]1 large tin of tomatoes[Enter]
Tomato puree to taste[Enter][Enter]
[Space][Tab]Method[Enter][Enter]
Preparation time[Tab][Tab]10 mins.[Tab][Tab]Cooking time[Tab][Tab]45 mins.[Enter][Enter]
1)[Tab]Parboil the rice with the stock cube in a small amount of water.[Enter]
Season the mince with the salt and sugar, and add the mixed spice.[Enter]
Mix the mince with the rice and butter.[Enter]
Hollow and stuff the courgettes, and place them in a large pan.[Enter]
Cover with the tomato sauce and season to taste.[Enter]
Cover the pan and simmer until tender--about 45 -- 60 mins.[Enter][Enter]
###[Enter]

The [**Space**] in the **For the sauce** sentence is necessary to prevent **AutoCorrect** from changing the subsequent [**Tab**] into a paragraph indentation – we want Word to treat it literally.

The completed recipe should now look like Figure 2.6:

˙Stuffed·Courgettes¶
¶

˙*Ingredients*¶
¶

˙For·the·stuffing¶
- · ¼·kg·minced·beef¶
- · 28g·butter¶
- · 1·cup·of·rice¶
- · 1·chicken·stock·cube¶
- · 4·tbsp.·Mixed·spice¶
- · Salt·and·**sugar**·to·taste¶
¶

˙For·the·sauce¶
- · 1·large·tin·of·tomatoes¶
- · Tomato·puree·to·taste¶
¶

˙*Method*¶
Preparation·time · · 10·mins. · · Cooking·time· · 45·mins.¶
¶
1) · Parboil·the·rice·with·the·stock·cube·in·a·small·amount·of·water.¶
2) · Season·the·mince·with·the·salt·and·sugar,·and·add·the·mixed·spice.¶
3) · Mix·the·mince·with·the·rice·and·butter.¶
4) · Hollow·and·stuff·the·courgettes,·and·place·them·in·a·large·pan.¶
5) · Cover·with·the·tomato·sauce·and·season·to·taste.¶
6) · Cover·the·pan·and·simmer·until·tender—about·45·-·60·mins.¶
¶

Figure 2.6: Result of AutoFormat when typing a recipe

Save the completed recipe as **Stuffed Courgettes.doc**.

AutoFormat for existing text

In addition to **AutoFormat As You Type**, it is possible to apply **AutoFormat** style changes to a whole document.

 From the menu, select **Tools, AutoCorrect Options**. Check that all of the **AutoFormat** options are ticked, as shown in Figure 2.7. Press **OK** to close the **AutoCorrect** dialogue.

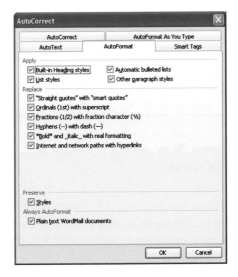

Figure 2.7: Options for AutoFormat

AutoFormat is Word's 'best guess' at the formatting styles that should be applied to a plain text document. In order to try it, we need a plain document; the easiest thing to do is to save a copy of the recipe file as a text file, so that all of the formatting information is thrown away.

 From the menu, select **File, Save As**. Choose **Plain text (*.txt)** as the **Save as type** (you will have to scroll down the list) and press **Save**.

Figure 2.8: Saving the recipe as plain text

The **File Conversion** dialogue is displayed, warning you that the formatting information will be lost. Press **OK**.

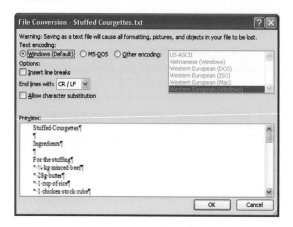

Figure 2.9: File Conversion dialogue

 From the menu, select **File**, **Close**.

 On the **File** menu, you should find that entry **1** in the recent file list is the text file you saved. Select this to open it. The text file loads. Notice that it is in the **Plain Text** style, with all of the formatting stripped out.

```
Stuffed·Courgettes¶
¶
Ingredients¶
¶
For·the·stuffing¶
*·¼·kg·minced·beef¶
*·28g·butter¶
*·1·cup·of·rice¶
*·1·chicken·stock·cube¶
*·4·tbsp.·Mixed·spice¶
*·Salt·and·sugar·to·taste¶
¶
For·the·sauce¶
*·1·large·tin·of·tomatoes¶
*·Tomato·puree·to·taste¶
¶
Method¶
Preparation·time·   ·   10·mins. ·   ·   Cooking·time   ·   ·   45·mins.
¶
1)·Parboil·the·rice·with·the·stock·cube·in·a·small·amount·of·water.¶
2)·Season·the·mince·with·the·salt·and·sugar,·and·add·the·mixed·spice.¶
3)·Mix·the·mince·with·the·rice·and·butter.¶
4)·Hollow·and·stuff·the·courgettes,·and·place·them·in·a·large·pan.¶
5)·Cover·with·the·tomato·sauce·and·season·to·taste.¶
6)·Cover·the·pan·and·simmer·until·tender—about·45·-·60·mins.¶
¶
¶
```

Figure 2.10: A plain text file

From the menu, select **Format, AutoFormat**.

 The **AutoFormat** dialogue is displayed. Select **AutoFormat now** and press **OK**.

˙**Stuffed·Courgettes**¶

˙**Ingredients**¶

For·the·stuffing¶
*·¼·kg·minced·beef¶

- · 28g·butter¶
- · 1·cup·of·rice¶
- · 1·chicken·stock·cube¶
- · 4·tbsp.·Mixed·spice¶
- · Salt·and·sugar·to·taste¶

¶

˙**For·the·sauce**¶

- · 1·large·tin·of·tomatoes¶
- · Tomato·puree·to·taste¶

¶

˙**Method**¶

Preparation·time · · 10·mins. ·   · Cooking·time·   · 45·mins.¶

1)·Parboil·the·rice·with·the·stock·cube·in·a·small·amount·of·water.¶
2)·Season·the·mince·with·the·salt·and·sugar,·and·add·the·mixed·spice.¶
3)·Mix·the·mince·with·the·rice·and·butter.¶
4)·Hollow·and·stuff·the·courgettes,·and·place·them·in·a·large·pan.¶
5)·Cover·with·the·tomato·sauce·and·season·to·taste.¶
6)·Cover·the·pan·and·simmer·until·tender—about·45·–·60·mins.¶
¶
¶

Figure 2.11: AutoFormatted document

As you can see, **AutoFormat** isn't perfect, but it does give you a head start when applying formatting to an unformatted document.

 Close **Stuffed Courgettes.txt** without saving, and reload the formatted file **Stuffed Courgettes.doc**.

Automatic text entry

Using AutoText

You can think of **AutoText** as a library of frequently used document fragments. This library allows you to insert recurring information (such as your address or a legal disclaimer) quickly into your documents.

AutoText entries are often just text, but you can use exactly the same method to create **AutoText** containing pictures or tables – simply select the part of the document you want to use as **AutoText**.

Creating new AutoText entries

In our recipe book example, there are lots of ingredients that we will be using repeatedly, so it may save some time to create **AutoText** entries for them.

 Select the text **1 large tin of tomatoes**. Select only the text, not the ¶ (paragraph) symbol that comes after it.

If you create **AutoText** from selected text that includes the ¶ (paragraph) symbol then the paragraph formatting (margins, etc.) is copied in addition to the character formatting.

 From the menu select **Insert, AutoText, New**.

 The **Create AutoText** dialogue is displayed. The **AutoText** name defaults to the phrase that was selected (type the rest if it is truncated). Press **OK**.

Figure 2.12: Creating AutoText

A new **AutoText** entry has been created. Test it by going to the end of the document and selecting **Insert, AutoText, Normal, 1 large tin of tomatoes**.

Rather than **Normal**, the new **AutoText** entry may be in a different category (based on the style of the original text). This doesn't matter.

 The phrase **1 large tin of tomatoes** appears in the document. Select **Edit, Undo Insert AutoText** from the menu to tidy up.

From now on, whenever you want to add the text **1 large tin of tomatoes** to an ingredients list in a recipe, you can do so using the **AutoText**. This saves some typing, but still takes a few clicks of the mouse.

However, there is some excellent news. Word uses **AutoText** entries to predict what you might be typing!

 Still at the end of the document, type **1 large**. A hint should appear, as shown in Figure 2.13. Instead of typing the rest of the phrase, just press **Enter**. The remaining words – **tin of tomatoes** – are added automatically.

1 large tin of tomatoes (Press ENTER to Insert)
1·la¶

Figure 2.13: AutoText completion hint

 Delete this new text to tidy up.

Test yourself

1. Create an **AutoCorrect** entry so that you can type **Ingred** instead of **Ingredients**.

2. Create **AutoText** entries for **minced beef** and **minced lamb**.

3. In a new blank document, try out each of the different types of **AutoCorrect** listed on page 24.

4. Find a long email or web page. **Save** it as plain text, then load it into Word and apply **AutoFormat**.

3 Styles and Templates

Introduction

In this chapter, we will create a village newsletter. This will be emailed to those villagers who have Internet access, and will be printed out and sold in the local shop. There will be one newsletter produced each month.

This chapter is all about ensuring consistency, both within a single document (by using **styles**) and across similar documents (by using **templates**). You will learn how using styles and templates will save you time when you later need to make changes to your documents.

In this chapter you will

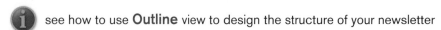 see how to use **Outline** view to design the structure of your newsletter

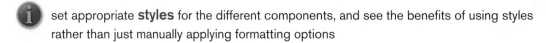 set appropriate **styles** for the different components, and see the benefits of using styles rather than just manually applying formatting options

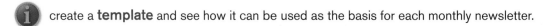 create a **template** and see how it can be used as the basis for each monthly newsletter.

Outline view

Word's document views

Microsoft Word gives you a choice of **views** you can use to look at your document.

Normal view shows the basic text without the fancy formatting options, and does not split it into pages. It is worth switching into this mode if you are working on a long or complicated document and find that your computer is operating very slowly. The name of this view is slightly misleading – nowadays you are more likely to do most of your work in **Print Layout** view (see below).

Web Layout view shows your document as it would appear if you exported it for use on the World Wide Web. As with **Normal** view, the document is not split into pages.

Print Layout view shows your document split into pages with all of the formatting applied. This is the view you will most often work in.

Reading Layout view displays your document in a form that is comfortable to read, using a large font and displaying one screen of information at a time. This is convenient if you want to read through a document, but is not that useful for editing.

Outline view uses the structure of the document to give you an overview and to let you quickly change the order of sections.

Using Outline view for planning

> **Syllabus Ref: AM3.1.2.6**
> Use outline options.

Because **Outline** view lets you focus on the structure of a document, and makes it very easy to change the order of the different sections, it is a good idea to use this view when planning a new document.

We are going to use **Outline** view to plan the structure of a monthly newsletter for the village of Stoke-by-Coombe.

 Open a new blank document.

 Switch to **Outline** view, either by selecting **View, Outline** from the menu or by pressing the **Outline View** button to the left of the horizontal scroll bar at the bottom of the window.

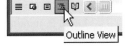

Type in the headings for the different sections of the newsletter, as shown in Figure 3.1. For now, they should all be in the **Heading 1** style (the default).

> **TIP**
>
> It can be useful to show the text styles in the left-hand column. To turn this feature on, select **Tools, Options** from the menu, and in the **View** tab set a value (such as **2 cm**) for the **Style area width**.

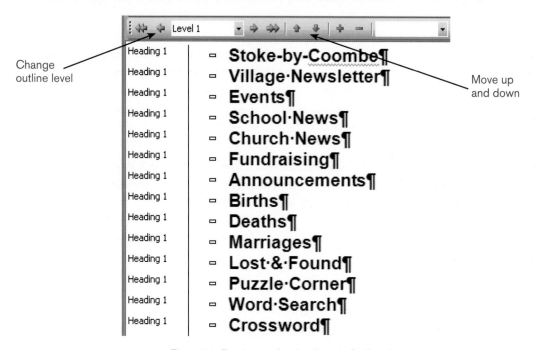

Figure 3.1: Entering section headings in Outline view

Notice the **Outlining** toolbar, as shown at the top of Figure 3.1, which should have appeared when you switched to **Outline** view. The green arrows let you change the level of the current line (for example, **Level 2** is a subheading within a **Level 1** section – we'll look at this next). The blue arrows let you move lines up and down; they flow through the other lines (again, we'll look at how this works).

Some of the lines you have entered need to be changed to subheadings; for example, **Fundraising** is a section within **Church News**.

 Position your insertion point anywhere in the **Fundraising** line and press the **single right green arrow** in the **Outlining** toolbar. This changes the **Fundraising** heading from Level 1 to Level 2, making it a subheading of the Level 1 heading above it (**Church News**).

Demote

Heading 1	▫ **School·News**¶
Heading 1	✛ **Church·News**¶
Heading 2	▫ *Fundraising*¶

Figure 3.2: Demoting the level of Fundraising

Notice that **Church News** now has a plus sign next to it, indicating the tree-like structure of the document. You can double-click the plus sign to **collapse** the tree, hiding the lower levels (in this case, **Fundraising**). Double-click again to reshow them.

There is a set of nifty keyboard shortcuts that you may find more efficient than the **Outlining** toolbar if you have to make a lot of changes to the structure of a document.

 Position your insertion point anywhere in the **Births** heading. Hold down both the **Shift** and **Alt** keys with your left hand, then use the arrow keys with your right hand: **left** and **right** increase and decrease the level, **up** and **down** move the location of the line. You can keep **Shift+Alt** pressed while you make more than one change to a line. You should be able to get the document looking like Figure 3.3 using only the keyboard. Try it!

Heading 1	▫ **Stoke-by-Coombe**¶
Heading 1	▫ **Village·Newsletter**¶
Heading 1	▫ **Events**¶
Heading 1	▫ **School·News**¶
Heading 1	✛ **Church·News**¶
Heading 2	▫ *Fundraising*¶
Heading 1	✛ **Announcements**¶
Heading 2	▫ *Births*¶
Heading 2	▫ *Deaths*¶
Heading 2	▫ *Marriages*¶
Heading 1	✛ **Puzzle·Corner**¶
Heading 2	▫ *Word·Search*¶
Heading 2	▫ *Crossword*¶
Heading 1	▫ **Lost·&·Found**¶

Figure 3.3: Newsletter structure

Styles

Syllabus Ref: AM3.1.1.8
Use available text design gallery options.

Now we have the structure for the newsletter, we can decide how we want it to look. We will control the formatting and behaviour of the different parts of the document by using **styles**.

> **TIP**
>
> By default, a new document has four styles: **Heading 1**, **Heading 2**, **Heading 3** and **Normal**. You may find you have more heading styles if you increased the level of any of the headings beyond 3 when you were experimenting with the layout – this doesn't matter.

 From the menu, select **Format, Styles and Formatting** to display the **Styles and Formatting** task pane. This shows the available styles and makes it easy to modify them.

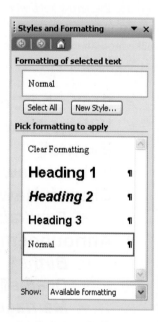

Figure 3.4: Styles and Formatting task pane

These default styles aren't very interesting. We can use Word's **Design Gallery** to import a set of styles from an existing template. (We'll be covering templates later in this chapter.)

From the menu, select **Format, Theme**. The **Theme** dialogue appears, as shown in Figure 3.5.

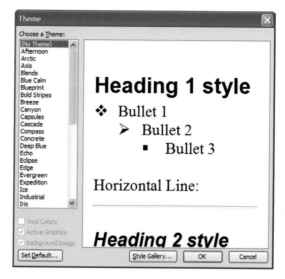

Figure 3.5: The Theme dialogue

 Click on a few of the different themes and watch the effect on the preview.

 We will not be changing the theme, just importing styles, so make sure that the top option **(No Theme)** is selected, then press the **Style Gallery** button at the bottom of the **Theme** dialogue. The **Style Gallery** appears.

 Select **Contemporary Report** from the **Template** list, as shown in Figure 3.6. Press **OK** to import the styles.

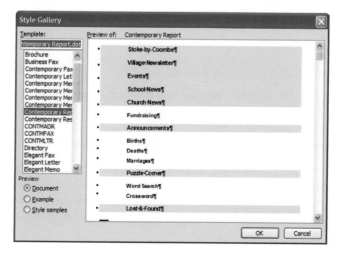

Figure 3.6: Importing styles from the Contemporary Report template

If you get the error **The feature you are trying to use is on a network resource that is unavailable** then the network server from which your office software was installed is no longer available. See http://support.microsoft.com/?kbid=828376

 Switch back to **Print Layout** view.

Your document should look like Figure 3.7. Notice that the **Heading 1** and **Heading 2** styles have been updated, and that there are now many more styles available in the **Styles and Formatting** task pane.

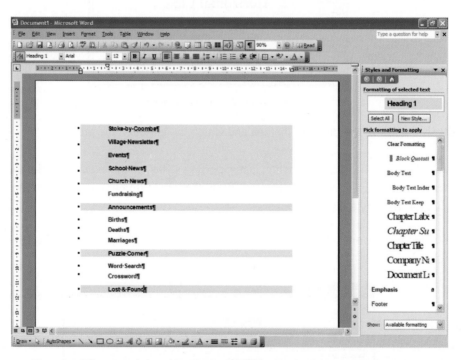

Figure 3.7: Village newsletter with styles imported from the Contemporary Report template

This is different from creating a document based on the **Contemporary Report** template (you will see later in this chapter how to do this). We have copied only the styles, not page setup options or anything else. Our document is still based on **Normal.dot** (the default Word template).

Another aspect of text design gallery options (**WordArt**) is covered in Chapter 8.

Modifying existing styles

Syllabus Ref: AM3.1.2.5

Modify existing character or paragraph styles.

 Place your insertion point anywhere in one of the **Heading 1** lines. The **Styles and Formatting** task pane should show **Heading 1** selected.

 Move your mouse over the **Heading 1** area at the top of the **Styles and Formatting** task pane. A down arrow appears on the right-hand side of the panel. Press this arrow to reveal a menu, as shown in Figure 3.8. Select **Modify**.

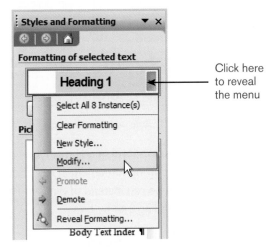

Figure 3.8: Modifying a style

This displays the **Modify Style** dialogue, which we will use to change the appearance of all of the main headings in our newsletter.

> There are two types of style: paragraph and character. **Paragraph styles** are applied to an entire paragraph and control things such as line spacing and margins. **Character styles** can override the formatting of any group of characters within a paragraph.
>
> So, for example, you might set up a paragraph style called **Instruction** that sets the general format for a numbered instruction list entry, and then create a character style called **Emphasis** that can be applied to individual words to make them stand out (for example, by making them red and bold).
>
> To modify an existing character style, you use exactly the same method as for modifying a paragraph style; the only difference you'll notice is exactly which formatting options Word will let you change for each.

 About half way down the **Modify Style** dialogue is a drop-down list of fonts. Change this to **Gill Sans Ultra Bold** (or some other font if you prefer).

Using the other controls on the same line in the **Formatting** area, set the font size to **18**, turn off bold formatting (**B**) and change the font colour to **dark blue**. The dialogue should then look like Figure 3.9(b). Press **OK**.

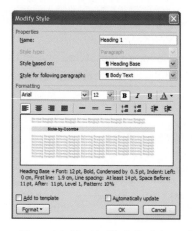 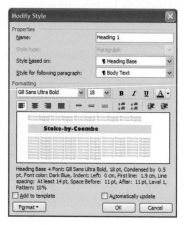

Figure 3.9: The Modify Style dialogue (a) before and (b) after making changes

The new style is applied to all of the top-level headings in the newsletter – this demonstrates the power of using styles rather than applying formatting styles directly as you go along. If you later decide that all the headings should be red instead of blue, you can simply make one change (to the style) instead of changing every heading one by one.

 Using the same method, change the **Heading 2** style to use size 16, bold, italic Tahoma in light blue. Make sure that you do not change the line with the insertion point to this new style by mistake – you should be modifying a style, not changing which styles are assigned to which lines.

Your document in **Print Layout** view should now look like Figure 3.10.

Figure 3.10: The headings with styles modified

Creating new styles

Syllabus Ref: AM3.1.2.4

Create new character or paragraph styles.

The two lines **Stoke-by-Coombe** and **Village Newsletter** are not really Level 1 headings, but are the title and the subtitle respectively. We'll create two new styles to make them stand out.

 Place your insertion point anywhere in the **Stoke-by-Coombe** line and press the **New Style** button in the **Styles and Formatting** task pane.

 In the **Name** field type **Newsletter Title**. Set **Style based on** to **Normal**. Set the font to **Old English Text MT** at size **48** and make it bold. Set the alignment to centred by pressing the **Center** button.

Center

 Press the **Format** button at the bottom of the dialogue and select **Font** to display the **Font** dialogue. Switch to the **Text Effects** tab and select **Sparkle Text**, as shown in Figure 3.11. Press **OK**.

Syllabus Ref: AM3.1.1.2

Apply animated text effect options.

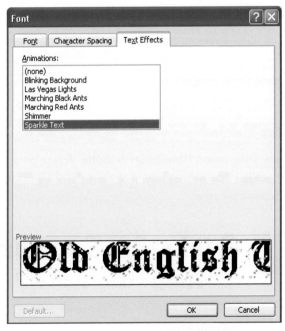

Figure 3.11: Setting an animated text effect

TIP

Animated text effects are not very professional. If you use them in real documents people are unlikely to take your document seriously.

However, it is in the ECDL syllabus, so you need to know how to do it!

The dialogue should look like Figure 3.12. Press **OK**.

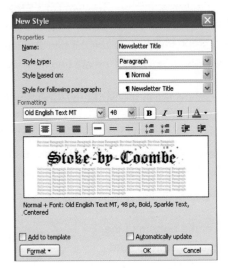

Figure 3.12: Creating a new style for the newsletter title

TIP

You can base styles on other styles; properties are inherited or overridden. Most new paragraph styles you create will be based on **Normal**.

 To apply this new style, select it from the **Pick formatting to apply** list in the **Styles and Formatting** task pane.

Create another new style, called **Newsletter Subtitle**. Again, base it on the **Normal** style. Select the **Lucida Handwriting** font, making it size **28** and centred. Set the **Village Newsletter** line to this new style.

Figure 3.13: Newsletter with styles applied

A style for the body text

The **Normal** style is the style on which all other styles are traditionally based. This means that if you wanted to make a document double-spaced, for example, you could modify the **Normal** style to have this setting, and all of the other styles would pick it up. Because of this, it is bad practice to use the **Normal** style directly in a document; we will use the built-in style **Body Text** instead.

 Place your insertion point at the end of the **Events** line and press **Enter** to create a new blank line. The style of this new line will be **Body Text**, because this was the setting in the **Style for following paragraph** option for the imported **Heading 1** style (see Figure 3.9 on page 44).

The **Heading 1** style uses **Normal** as the default **Style for following paragraph**.

However, the **Heading 1** style in the **Contemporary Report** template uses **Body Text** as the **Style for following paragraph**. Because we used the **Style Gallery** to import these styles, we picked up this more useful setting.

 Enter some sample text: **A car boot sale will be held in the upper field on 6th August. Contact Tim Collins for details.**

Borders and shading

Syllabus Ref: AM3.1.2.1
Use paragraph shading options.

Syllabus Ref: AM3.1.2.2
Use paragraph border options.

It would look good to have each announcement in its own shaded box, so we'll create a style for this.

 Again, we'll start by creating some sample text to work with. Position your insertion point at the end of the **Births** line and press **Enter**. On the new line type **Sarah Jane Timmons was born to Maria and John Timmons of Steep Hill on 29th June. Sarah weighed 10 pounds, 6 ounces.**

 Press the **New Style** button in the **Styles and Formatting** task pane. Call the style **Body Text Box** and base it on the **Body Text** style.

 Press the **Format** button and select **Border** to display the **Borders and Shading** dialogue.

In the **Borders** tab, select the **Shadow** setting (see Figure 3.14). This will add a drop shadow to paragraphs of the new style.

In the **Shading** tab, select the colour **Tan** (the second one from the left on the bottom row – see Figure 3.15). This will give a tan background to our boxes. Press **OK** to return to the **New Style** dialogue.

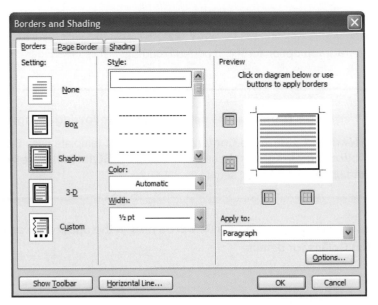

Figure 3.14: The Borders and Shading dialogue, Borders tab

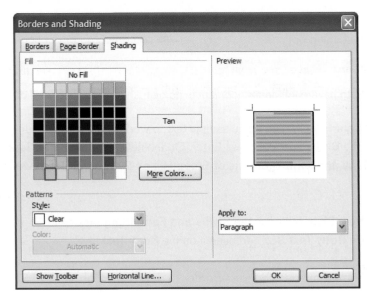

Figure 3.15: The Borders and Shading dialogue, Shading tab

The **New Style** dialogue should now look like Figure 3.16. Press **OK**.

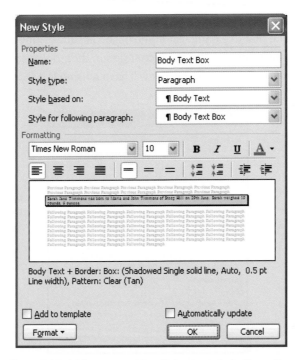

Figure 3.16: Adding a new style with border and shading options

 Set the sample birth text to this new style.

Character styles

So far, all of the styles we have used have been **paragraph styles**. This means that they apply to whole paragraphs and control both font and paragraph formatting. Every paragraph in a document must have one paragraph style.

Sometimes you want to be able to apply a style to only a portion of a paragraph. Word has a different type of style, called **character styles**, to do this. Unlike **paragraph styles**, **character styles** cannot be used to change things like paragraph spacing and tab stops.

Everyone likes to see his or her name in print! We'll create a new character style that we can use to highlight all of the names in the newsletter.

 Press the **New Style** button in the **Styles and Formatting** task pane. Enter a **Name** of **Name Highlight** and make sure the **Style type** is set to **Character**. Make the font bold and dark red.

 Since you will want to be able to quickly apply this style to selected text, it makes sense to assign a shortcut key to it. Press the **Format** button (notice how some of the options are unavailable, because this is a **character style**) and select **Shortcut Key**. Press the **Alt** and **N** keys together (notice that this particular combination is **[unassigned]**, so you are not hiding some other command). Change the **Save changes in** drop-down to the current document. If you have not saved your document yet, it will have a name like **Document1**. Press **Assign**, then **Close**.

Figure 3.17: Assigning a shortcut key to the Name Highlight style

 The **New Style** dialogue should look like Figure 3.18. Press **OK** to close it.

Figure 3.18: Creating a character style

There are three ways to assign this new style to selected text. We'll quickly run through them.

 Highlight the text **Tim Collins** in the **Events** sample text, then press **Alt+N**. The name should become red and bold.

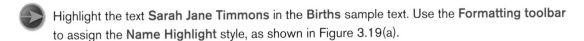 Highlight the text **Sarah Jane Timmons** in the **Births** sample text. Use the **Formatting toolbar** to assign the **Name Highlight** style, as shown in Figure 3.19(a).

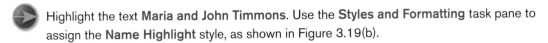 Highlight the text **Maria and John Timmons**. Use the **Styles and Formatting** task pane to assign the **Name Highlight** style, as shown in Figure 3.19(b).

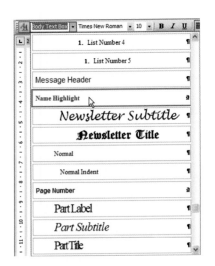

Figure 3.19: Two ways to assign a style: (a) the Formatting toolbar, (b) the Styles and Formatting task pane

For the final stage, we want to set up the newsletter to have a 2-column layout.

Columns

Syllabus Ref: AM3.2.4.1
Create multiple column layouts.

You may have noticed that all of our styles indent the text by about 2 cm. This comes from the Contemporary Report's **Normal** style, but is not really suitable for a multiple column layout. We'll turn this indentation off first.

 Modify the **Normal** style. In the **Modify Style** dialogue, press the **Decrease Indent** button repeatedly until all of the text in the preview is flush left. Then press **OK** to apply the change.

Decrease Indent

This removes the indent from everything apart from the **Heading 1 style**, which has an overridden first line indent. We'll turn this off.

 Modify the **Heading 1** style. In the **Modify Style** dialogue, select **Format**, **Paragraph**. In the **Paragraph** dialogue, change the **Indentation** section's **Special** setting to **(none)**, as shown in Figure 3.20. Press **OK** for each of the dialogues to apply the change.

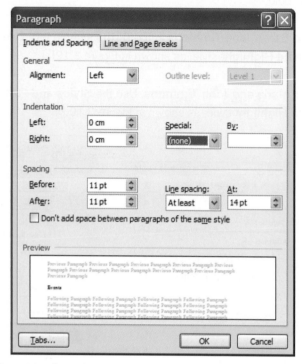

Figure 3.20: Removing the first line indentation from the Heading 1 style

 The easy way to change the number of columns is to click the **Columns** button in the **Standard** toolbar and then click on **2 Columns**, as shown in Figure 3.21.

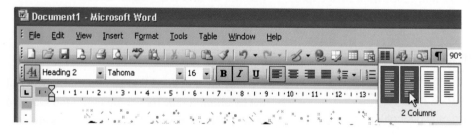

Figure 3.21: Setting 2-column layout

 TIP

You can select **Format**, **Columns** from the menu to display a dialogue that gives you a finer control over the widths of the columns. See Chapter 4, page 72.

The newsletter should now look like Figure 3.22.

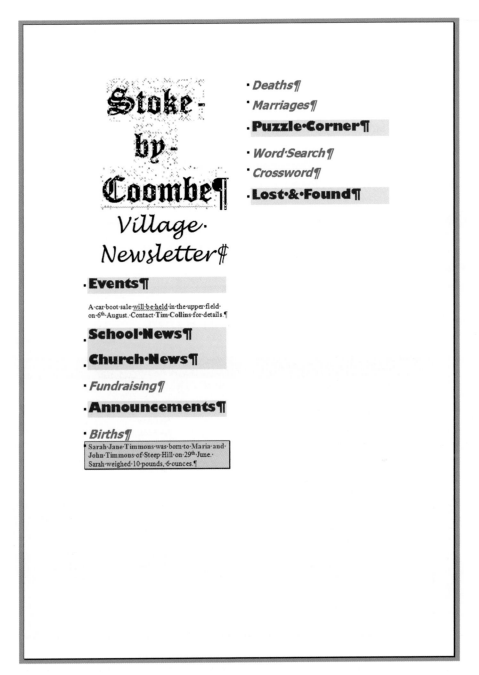

Figure 3.22: Newsletter with formatting applied

Templates

In Word, a template is a document that is used as the basis for other documents. This is exactly what we have been creating with the newsletter.

 From the menu select **File, Save As**. The **Save As** dialogue appears.

 Change the **Save as type** to **Document Template (*.dot)**. Word automatically changes to the folder on your PC where it stores the document templates.

TIP

You can open any template or document, make any changes you need, and then use **File, Save As** to save it as a new template.

 Set the **File name** to **Stoke newsletter.dot** and press **Save**.

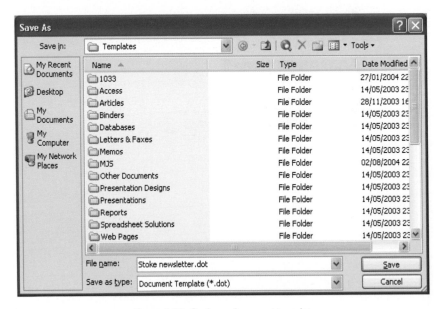

Figure 3.23: Saving a document template

 From the menu, select **File, Close**.

Now it's easy to create a new newsletter each month.

From the menu, select **File, New**. The **New Document** task pane will appear.

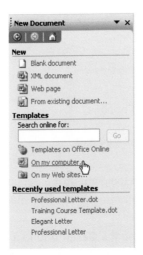

Figure 3.24: New Document task pane

 Select **On my computer** to open the **Templates** dialogue.

 Select **Stoke newsletter.dot** and make sure that **Create New** is set to **Document** (see Figure 3.25). Press **OK** to create the newsletter.

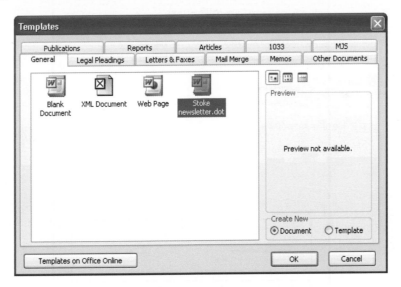

Figure 3.25: Creating a new document from a template

 Save the new newsletter as **June Newsletter.doc** in the location where you have been saving your work, and then close the document.

Modifying an existing template

Sometimes it's useful to make changes to an existing template. This is just as easy as modifying a document.

> **Syllabus Ref: AM3.1.3.1**
> Change basic formatting and layout options in a template.

Open the **Stoke newsletter.dot** template (**not** a document based on it). It is probably listed in the **recently used file list** at the bottom of the **File** menu, which is the quickest way to reopen it.

Modify the **Body Text** style to use the **Garamond** font at size **12**.

Modify the **Body Text Box** style, editing its **Paragraph** options (via the **Format** button). In the **Paragraph** dialogue, make sure the **Line and Page Breaks** tab is selected and tick the box for **Keep lines together**, as shown in Figure 3.26. Press **OK** to confirm the change.

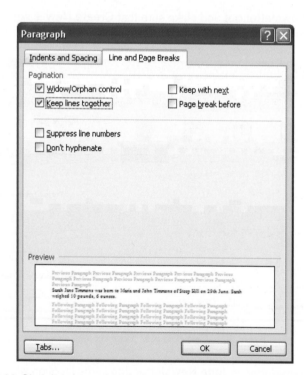

Figure 3.26: Changing paragraph options so that paragraphs will not split across pages

It is important that you understand the meaning of each of the options on the **Line and Page Breaks** tab.

In publishing, a **widow** occurs when the last line of a paragraph appears on its own at the top of a page; the corresponding term for the first line of a paragraph appearing at the bottom of a page is **orphan**. It is a good idea to avoid both of these problems in the documents you produce. If you tick the **Widow/Orphan control** box, Word will automatically keep paragraphs together to prevent widows and orphans (although it will still allow two or more lines from a paragraph to appear at the top or bottom of a page).

The box **Keep lines together** goes one stage further by preventing the paragraph from being split at all. If a paragraph with this option set is too long to fit at the bottom of a page, the whole paragraph will be moved to the top of the next page.

The **Keep with next** option is typically used for headings. If set for a paragraph, it prevents a page break from splitting it from the paragraph that follows it.

You can use **Page break before** if text of a certain style, such as **Heading 1**, should always start a new page. However, it is usually better to use **sections** (see page 68) to control page breaks.

The last two options allow you to override line numbering and hyphenation for particular styles, even if these options are turned on for the rest of the document.

The **Modify Style** dialogue should look like Figure 3.27. Press **OK**.

Test adding a paragraph of text in the **Body Text Box** style to the bottom of the first column. Confirm that when the paragraph gets too long to fit, it is moved to the top of the right-hand column. Once you're happy with how the **Keep lines together** option works, delete the new paragraph you've just created.

Save and close the template.

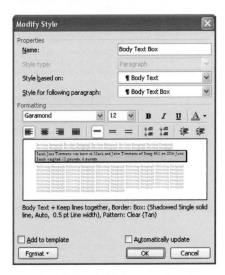

Figure 3.27: Modified paragraph style

Test yourself

1. Using **Outline** view, change the newsletter template by adding two new Level 2 headings – **Nursery** and **Primary** – below **School News**.

2. Create a new character style called **Stoke Highlight**. It should apply the **Old English Text MT** font.

3. Create an **AutoCorrect** entry that detects when you have typed **SBC**, and changes it to **Stoke-by-Coombe** with the **Stoke Highlight** character style applied.

TIP

Start by creating the style, typing **Stoke-by-Coombe** somewhere in the template, and applying the style to it.

- **Deaths¶**
- **Marriages¶**
- **Puzzle·Corner¶**
- **Word·Search¶**
- **Crossword¶**
- **Lost·&·Found¶**

·Events¶

A car boot sale will be held in the upper · field on 6ᵗʰ August. Contact Tim · Collins for details.¶

An AutoCorrect entry has been added · that lets you type SBC to get it · automatically changed to 𝕾𝖙𝖔𝖐𝖊·𝖇𝖞· 𝕮𝖔𝖔𝖒𝖇𝖊.¶

·School·News¶

- **Nursery¶**
- **Primary¶**
- **Church·News¶**
- **Fundraising¶**
- **Announcements¶**
- **Births¶**

Sarah Jane Timmons was born to · Maria and John Timmons of Steep · Hill on 29ᵗʰ June. Sarah weighed 10 · pounds, 6 ounces.¶

Figure 3.28: The template after completing the exercises

4 Document Structure

Introduction

This chapter deals with the physical structure of documents. You will see how to use **master documents** to bring together separate documents into a book, and how **sections** within documents give you control over layout.

In this chapter you will

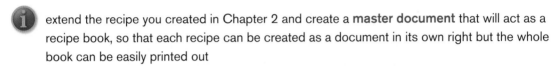

extend the recipe you created in Chapter 2 and create a **master document** that will act as a recipe book, so that each recipe can be created as a document in its own right but the whole book can be easily printed out

partition the recipe book into **sections**; these give you greater control over layout and page numbering

see how to create and control **multiple columns** of text.

Master documents

Here is an example scenario in which a **master document** might be useful.

Suppose that a large company wants to produce a printed telephone directory that contains contact details for its entire staff. This directory will need a title page and table of contents, followed by the directory (department by department), and finally an alphabetical index by surname. Each department has a secretary who will be in charge of keeping the details for staff in that department up to date.

You can think of a **master document** as a book where some of the pages have been torn out and replaced by a note saying 'for details, refer to document such-and-such'. The advantage of Word over this physical example, however, is that the 'torn out' pages still *appear* to be in the book: you can edit the **subdocument** (the extracted pages) and the changes will be reflected in the **master document**. When you print out the **master document**, all of the **subdocuments** will be printed too. Even better, page numbering will flow logically throughout, and any tables of content or indexes will apply to the whole lot: the **master document** and any **subdocuments** it contains.

The telephone directory example is ideally suited to a **master document**. A single document can be created with pointers to each of the departments' telephone directory **subdocuments**. A table of contents and index added to this **master document** would refer to all of the contact details, and update whenever they were changed. Individual departments could choose to print out just the **subdocument** for their own department. If they wanted a better-looking internal directory, they could create their own **master document**, referring to the same **subdocument**, and format it as they wished.

Don't worry if you've found this difficult to follow: it should become clear with an example. We're going to create a recipe book **master document** and add the individual recipes as **subdocuments**.

Creating a recipe book

Do you remember that in Chapter 2 you wrote a recipe for stuffed courgettes? Now you're going to create a new document to act as the 'binder' (**master document**) to hold all of your recipes (**subdocuments**) together.

Create a new document and switch it into **Outline** view.

 Create the following Level 1 headings: **Contents, Starters, Main Courses, Desserts, Index.**

Introducing the master document buttons from the **Outlining** toolbar:

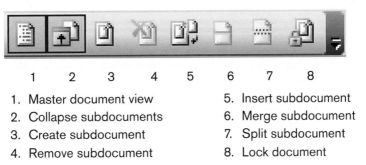

1. Master document view	5. Insert subdocument
2. Collapse subdocuments	6. Merge subdocument
3. Create subdocument	7. Split subdocument
4. Remove subdocument	8. Lock document

Figure 4.1: Master document toolbar buttons

 We want to add the preface, created in Chapter 2, after the contents. Position your insertion point to the left of the first **S** in **Starters** and press the **Insert subdocument** button (5 in Figure 4.1).

 Locate the **Preface.doc** file you saved when you were working on Chapter 2. Click on it and press **Open**.

Your document should now look like Figure 4.2. Notice the light grey box that has been draw around the subdocument, which has now become part of the tree (you can expand and collapse its branches by double-clicking on its plus/minus signs, just as you can for any other part of the document). In effect you can now treat the preface as if it were part of this new master document, even though any changes you make to it will be stored in its original file. If you update **Preface.doc** directly, you will see the changes reflected in this **master document** the next time you open it.

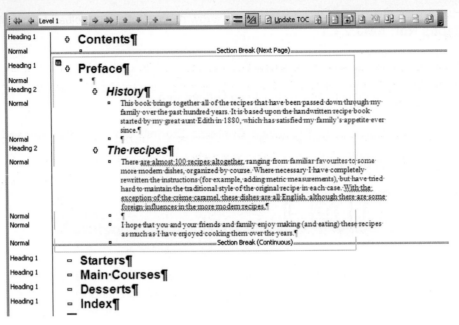

Figure 4.2: Master document with a subdocument

The other existing document we want to add to the recipe book is the recipe for stuffed courgettes, also created in Chapter 2.

 Position your insertion point at the beginning of the **Desserts** line (so that we are inserting into the **Main Courses** section) and press the **Insert Subdocument** button.

 Navigate to **Stuffed Courgettes.doc**, select it and click **Open**.

It is just as easy to remove a subdocument from a master document. Click anywhere in the subdocument and then press **Remove Subdocument** (icon 4 in Figure 4.1). This breaks the link between the master document and the subdocument, but leaves the subdocument's content in the master document. You can then delete the content that came from the subdocument, or edit it in any way you see fit, without altering the original subdocument.

To delete a subdocument in a single step, click its **Subdocument** icon (see the following step) and then press the **Delete** key.

The recipe is added to the book, but notice how the heading **Stuffed Courgettes** is in **Heading 1** style, putting it at the same level as the **Main Courses** section that it is supposed to be in. The easiest way to fix this is as follows.

  Click the **Subdocument** icon, which is located at the top left of the recipe. This will select the entire recipe, so that we can treat it as a unit.

Sub-
document

Press the **Tab** key (or the single right green arrow on the **Outlining** toolbar) to demote all of the text.

You will find that the recipe's heading is now Level 2, and all of its subheadings have been changed accordingly. We don't want a page break between the **Main Courses** heading and the **Stuffed Courgettes** recipe, so we will change the type of section break.

 With your text insertion point in the **Stuffed Courgettes** recipe, select **File, Page Setup** from the main menu. The **Page Setup** dialogue appears. In the **Layout** tab, change **Section start** to **Continuous** and make sure that **Apply to** is set to **This section**, as shown in Figure 4.3. Press **OK** to apply the change.

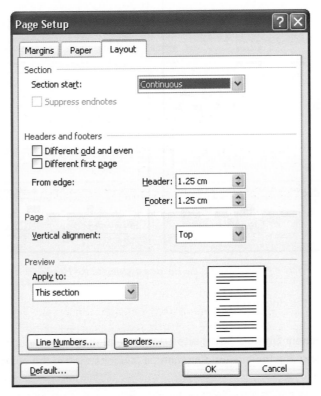

Figure 4.3: Page setup dialogue with Continuous selected

 This is an appropriate stage to save the file, so do so, calling it **Recipe Book.doc**.

If you're quick, you'll see that **two disk icons** appear briefly in the **status bar** at the bottom of the window (you normally get only one when saving a 'normal' document). This shows that Word is saving both the master document and the changes that you made to the recipe (the changes to the heading levels).

two disk icons

Master documents and styles

Remember that in Chapter 3 we used **document styles** to apply a consistent look and feel to similar pieces of text spread throughout a document (for example, making all of the Level 1 headings use the Gill Sans Ultra Bold font in the village newsletter).

 Change the **Heading 1** style so that it uses size 22 underlined text (see Figure 4.4(a)).

 Change the **Heading 2** style so that it uses size 18 text, and turn off the italics. From the **Format** menu, select **Font** and choose the option for **Small caps** (see Figure 4.4(b)).

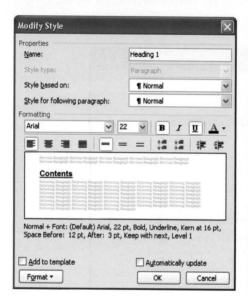 

Figure 4.4: Modifying (a) the Heading 1 style, (b) the Heading 2 style

 Save and close the document.

 Open the document **Stuffed Courgettes.doc**. Notice that, even though you modified the style for **Heading 2** in the master document, it is unchanged in the subdocument.

Note!

This is an important and powerful feature – when you modify styles in a master document, it overrides those styles but does not change them in the original subdocuments.

 Close the recipe and reopen the master document (**Recipe Book.doc**).

The master document will open with its subdocuments compressed, as shown in Figure 4.5. You can use the **Expand/Collapse Documents** button to toggle between the two views.

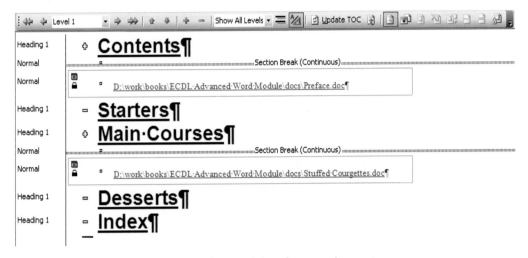

Figure 4.5: Collapsed view of a master document

Creating a subdocument

You can create a new subdocument directly from inside a master document. In this case, we'll add a new recipe (for a boiled egg, which should save you some typing) from inside the recipe book.

> **Syllabus Ref: AM3.2.1.2**
> Create a subdocument based on heading styles within a master document.

 Make sure the subdocuments are expanded (you can't create new subdocuments unless the existing subdocuments are being displayed) and position your insertion point at the start of the **Desserts** line.

 You create a new subdocument from a heading, so press **Enter**, move up to the new blank line, and type **Boiled Egg**. Set this to the **Heading 2** style (you can just press the **Tab** key, since you're in **Outline** view).

 With the text insertion point still in the **Boiled Egg** line, press the **Create Subdocument** button.

A new subdocument is created between two section breaks (see Figure 4.6). Notice the grey subdocument box that now goes around the 'Boiled Egg' section.

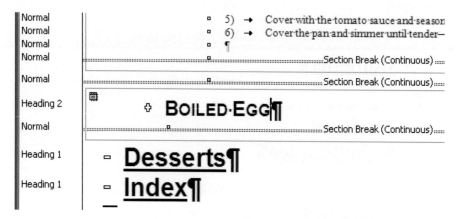

Figure 4.6: A new subdocument added between section breaks

 Switch to **Print Layout** view (just because it's easier to work with text in this view than in **Outline** view) and enter the new recipe as shown in Figure 4.7.

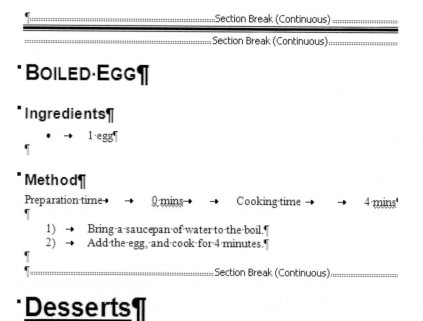

Figure 4.7: Adding the Boiled Egg recipe as a subdocument

 Switch back to **Outline** view and press the **Collapse Subdocuments** button. You will get a warning dialogue asking if you want to save the changes to the master document – just click **OK**.

Notice how a new subdocument, named after the heading you selected, has been created in the same directory as the recipe book, and has been embedded as a link.

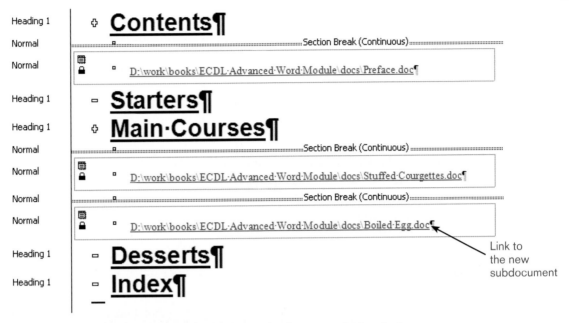

Figure 4.8: The new subdocument has been created automatically

Editing a subdocument

Although you can edit the contents of subdocuments by expanding them all inside the master document, sometimes it will be more convenient to make changes to one document at a time (for example, if the expanded master document is very large). There are three ways to open a subdocument for editing:

The subdocuments still exist as documents on disk, independent of the master document. You can open and edit them just as you would any other document – the changes will become part of the master document the next time you open that.

You can open a subdocument from the master document by holding down the **Ctrl** key and clicking on the subdocument's hyperlink. This will open the subdocument in a new window. If you hover over a hyperlink, Word will even remind you of this shortcut!

Double-clicking the **Subdocument** icon in the top-left of each subdocument will also open it for editing.

Sub-document

Use one of the last two of these methods to open **Boiled Egg.doc** from within **Recipe Book.doc**.

Because **Boiled Egg.doc** was created from inside the recipe book, it has picked up its style definitions (i.e. the **Heading 2** style uses **small caps**).

➤ Add a second ingredient (**2 slices of bread**) and a third method step (**Toast the bread and serve with the egg**).

➤ Save and close **Boiled Egg.doc**.

➤ Back in **Recipe Book.doc**, expand the subdocuments. Notice how the changes you made to the boiled egg recipe have been incorporated.

➤ Save **Recipe Book.doc**.

Sections

You may have noticed that Word adds **section breaks** before and after each of the subdocuments in a master document. The use of sections is much more general than that, but this is a convenient place to look at what they are and how to use them.

You use a **section** to mark out a portion of a document for special treatment. The main uses are as follows.

ⓘ All of the **Page Setup** options can be applied to an individual section, meaning that you can change **margin** settings, the **paper size** or **orientation** (whether it is **portrait** or **landscape**) wherever you need to.

ⓘ You can change the starting number and format of **page numbers**. This is commonly used to create a document with front matter numbered using roman numerals, followed by the main body restarting its numbering at 1 in digits.

ⓘ You can use sections to control **page breaks**, for example forcing each chapter of a book to start on a new page.

ⓘ **Multi-column layouts** can be constrained by sections.

We are going to use sections to improve the recipe book in two ways: first, we'll put the Contents and Preface into a section with roman numerals for the page numbers; then, we'll add a two-column section for the index.

Setting page numbers for the front matter

You create a new section by inserting a **section break** into the appropriate place in your document; everything before the **section break** becomes one section, everything after it becomes another.

We want to group the Contents and Preface together with roman numerals as the page numbers, so we need to insert a new **section break** between the Preface subdocument and the Starters heading.

 Ensure that the subdocuments are expanded and switch to **Print Layout** view.

We want each Level 1 heading to start on a new page – the easiest way to achieve this is with a quick tweak to the style of **Heading 1**.

 Modify the **Heading 1** style. Change the paragraph format (via the **Format** button) so that **Page Break Before** is set (it's on the **Line and Page Breaks** tab – see Figure 4.9).

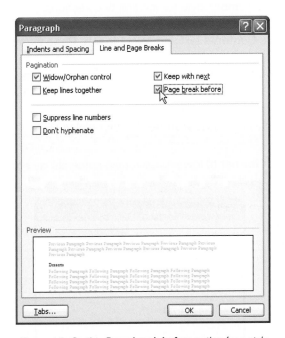

*Figure 4.9: Setting **Page break before** option for a style*

The recipe book (in its compressed form) should now have six pages: **Contents**, **Preface**, **Starters**, **Main Courses**, **Desserts** and **Index**.

Notice that there are some **continuous section breaks** already in the document, which were added automatically before each of the subdocuments. These can be safely ignored – we won't apply any special formatting to these sections.

The first step in setting up our two different formats of page numbering is to display some page numbers for the recipe book.

From the menu, select **Insert**, **Page Numbers**.

 Change the **Alignment** to **Center** and press **OK**. Your six pages should now be numbered 1–6 at the bottom of each.

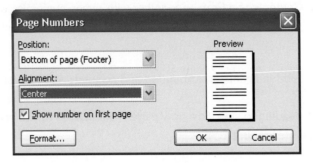

Figure 4.10: Adding page numbers

We want to change the page number style for the first two sections.

 Click anywhere in the **Contents** text and select **Insert**, **Page Numbers** from the menu.

Note that we aren't inserting anything, despite the name of the menu, merely replacing what's already there.

 Click **Format** to display the **Page Number Format** dialogue.

 Change the **Number format** to lower case roman numerals, as shown in Figure 4.11, and press **OK**.

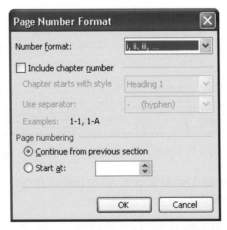

Figure 4.11: Changing the style of page numbers

Press **OK** to close the **Page Numbers** dialogue.

 Repeat this process with your text insertion point in the **Preface** section.

Your first three pages should now be numbered **i**, **ii** and **3** respectively. This is part of the job done, but the numbering of the main body of the book ought to restart from 1.

 Position your insertion point anywhere in the **Starters** title and display the **Page Number Format** dialogue again.

 This time, select **Start at** and change its value to **1**. Accept the change (press **OK** on both dialogues).

Now your page numbers should run in the sequence: **i, ii, 1, 2, 3, 4.**

Syllabus Ref: AM3.2.3.2
Delete section breaks in a document.

 TIP

It's easy to delete section breaks from a document: position the insertion point just before the section break and press **Delete**. Remember this – you may be asked to do it in the exam.

Syllabus Ref: AM3.2.3.1
Create sections in a document.

Columns of text

The final change in this chapter is to add a 3-column section for the index.

 Position your insertion point at the end of the **Index** title and press **Enter** a couple of times to create some blank lines.

 TIP

If you insert the section break when the cursor is on the title line itself, you will get some strange behaviour. This is because the section break is given the style of the line you are on when you create it. Now, our **Heading 1** style has **page break before** set, so the section break would position itself at the top of the next page!

Position your insertion point on the first blank line below the **Index** title. We want to insert a **continuous section break** here so that the body of the index can be set up to have three columns without affecting the rest of the book. From the menu select **Insert, Break**.

The **Break** dialogue will be displayed.

 Select **Continuous** – for a section that does not start a new page – and press **OK**.

Figure 4.12: Inserting a continuous section break

 Position your insertion point just before the new section break and change its style to **Normal** (if it isn't already), as shown in Figure 4.13.

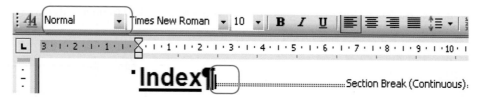

Figure 4.13: Insertion point positioned just before the newly added section break

Syllabus Ref: AM3.2.4.1
Create multiple column layouts.

 With your insertion point on one of the blank lines below your new section break, set the page to use three columns. The easy way to do this is to click on the **Columns** button (on the **Standard** toolbar) and, keeping your mouse button down, drag across three columns, as shown in Figure 4.14. Then release the mouse button.

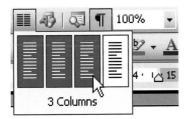

Figure 4.14: Setting a three-column layout

Notice how the **ruler bar** has changed. It should now have three white areas, indicating the three columns.

Figure 4.15: Ruler bar showing three columns

Let's add some text so you can see the three columns in action.

 On the first blank line below the **Index** heading, type **Index me**.

 Select the words you have just typed, but not the paragraph symbol at the end of the line. (Use the keyboard for this by holding down **Shift** and using the **arrow keys**; you might not be able to avoid the paragraph mark using the mouse.) When you have selected the words, press **Ctrl+C** to copy them to the clipboard.

 Now we want to paste this sentence into the document lots of times to flesh out the page. Press **Ctrl+V** repeatedly until you have filled all three columns with text. You can hold down **Ctrl** with your left hand and tap **V** with your right. Your index page should look like Figure 4.16.

˙Index¶ ···Section Break (Continuous)···

Index·me.·Index·me.·Index·me.·Index·me.·Index·me.·
Index·me.·Index·me.·Index·me.·Index·me.·Index·me.·
Index·me.·Index·me.·Index·me.·Index·me.·Index·me.·
Index·me.·Index·me.·Index·me.·Index·me.·Index·me.·
Index·me.·Index·me.·Index·

Index·me.·Index·me.·Index·me.·Index·me.·Index·me.·
Index·me.·Index·me.·Index·me.·Index·me.·Index·me.·
Index·me.·Index·me.·Index·me.·Index·me.·Index·me.·
Index·me.·Index·me.·Index·me.·Index·me.·Index·me.·
Index·me.·Index·me.·Index·

Index·me.·Index·me.·Index·me.·Index·me.·Index·me.·
Index·me.·Index·me.·Index·me.·Index·me.·Index·me.·
Index·me.·Index·me.·Index·me.·Index·me.·Index·me.·
Index·me.·Index·me.·Index·me.·Index·me.·Index·me.·
Index·me.·Index·me.·Index·

Figure 4.16: Three column layout

TIP

Word has a built-in function for generating placeholder text: **=rand(p,s)** where **p** is the number of paragraphs to generate and **s** is the number of sentences per paragraph. You could try typing **=rand(3,4)** in a blank document – you should get three paragraphs, each with four sets of **The quick brown fox jumped over the lazy dog.**

Using the **Columns** toolbar button is the easy way to create multi-column layouts. You can get finer control over the width and spacing of the individual columns by using the **Columns** dialogue.

 With your insertion point in one of the columns, select **Format**, **Columns** from the menu.

Syllabus Ref: AM3.2.4.2
Modify column layouts.

 Select the preset **Two**, as shown in Figure 4.17. This defaults the settings to a layout with two 6.7 cm columns separated by a 1.25 cm gap. Press **OK**.

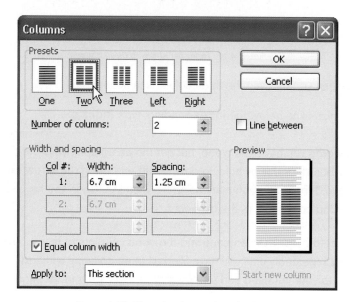

Figure 4.17: Changing the number of columns

Your index should now have two columns instead of three. There is quite a generous gap between the columns: let's reduce the gap and add a separating line.

Syllabus Ref: AM3.2.4.3
Modify column width and spacing.

 Display the **Columns** dialogue again. Increase the width of column 1 to **6.95 cm** – the spacing will automatically shrink to **0.75 cm** to compensate. Tick the **Line between** box and press **OK**.

 TIP

Notice how, because the **Equal column width** box is ticked, you need to change only one of the column widths; if you want to set disproportionate columns (like the **Left** and **Right** presets) simply untick this box.

Don't worry if you get a value other than **0.75 cm** – it just means your paper or margins are set up differently.

The index should now look like Figure 4.18.

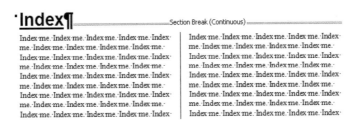

Figure 4.18: The result of modifying the column settings

Syllabus Ref: AM3.2.4.4

Insert a column break.

Sometimes it is useful to be able to insert a **column break**, which marks the end of a column so that the text that follows it starts at the top of the next column.

 Place your insertion point somewhere in the middle of the first column of 'index me' text.

 From the menu, select **Insert**, **Break**. Remember that this is the same method used to insert **section breaks** – instead, select **Column break**, as shown in Figure 4.19, and press **OK**.

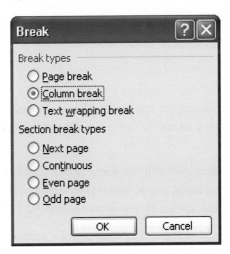

Figure 4.19: Inserting a column break

This should force the text following the **column break** to jump to the top of the next column, as shown in Figure 4.20.

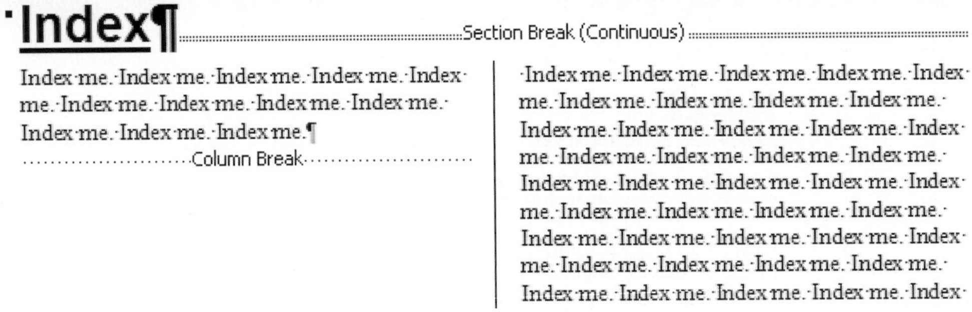

·Index¶ ················Section Break (Continuous)·················

Index·me.·Index·me.·Index·me.·Index·me.·Index·
me.·Index·me.·Index·me.·Index·me.·Index·me.·
Index·me.·Index·me.·Index·me.¶
·····················Column Break·····················

·Index·me.·Index·me.·Index·me.·Index·me.·Index·
me.·Index·me.·Index·me.·Index·me.·Index·me.·
Index·me.·Index·me.·Index·me.·Index·me.·Index·
me.·Index·me.·Index·me.·Index·me.·Index·me.·
Index·me.·Index·me.·Index·me.·Index·me.·Index·
me.·Index·me.·Index·me.·Index·me.·Index·me.·
Index·me.·Index·me.·Index·me.·Index·me.·Index·
me.·Index·me.·Index·me.·Index·me.·Index·me.·
Index·me.·Index·me.·Index·me.·Index·me.·Index·

Figure 4.20: A column break

> **Syllabus Ref: AM3.2.4.5**
> Delete a column break.

It's just as easy to delete it again.

 Position your insertion point just before the column break and press the **Delete** key. You will probably have to delete the paragraph symbol too, so that the lines join back together.

Congratulations! You now know how to use **master documents** to split up long tomes, how to use **sections** to hive off parts of your documents for special formatting, and how to apply and modify **multi-column layouts**.

 Don't forget to save **Recipe Book.doc**.

Test yourself

1. Create a new blank master document (do not use the recipe book or any of its subdocuments)and experiment using the options to **Merge subdocument**, **Split subdocument** and **Lock document**.

2. Use **sections** to create a document that has some pages in **portrait orientation** and some in **landscape**. (Hint: To add the blank pages, use **Insert**, **Break** and select **Next page** section breaks. Use **File**, **Page Setup** to change the page orientation.)

3. Create a new blank document with a three-column layout; make the centre column much wider than the two side columns. Experiment with typing in some of the text from this book, with syllabus references in the left-hand column and tips in the right-hand one, using **column breaks** where necessary.

4. Create a template called **Book.dot**, based on the recipe book. It should comprise three sections: **Contents**, **Chapter 1** (empty – you will need to create this) and **Index**. The **Contents** page should be numbered **A**, with **Chapter 1** and **Index** being **1** and **2**.

5 Cross-References

Introduction

This chapter deals with topics that are all connected in some way with cross-referencing; in other words, references to information held elsewhere in a document. We will be expanding on the recipe book example and creating a letter.

In this chapter you will

add a **table of contents** and an **index** to the recipe book

bookmark one of the recipes, and see how **bookmarks** can be used to speed up navigation through long documents and as targets for **cross-references**

learn how to add information to a document by using **fields**

create **footnotes** and see how to update and move them.

Contents and indexes

Tables of content

The first thing we're going to do is to add a table of contents to the recipe book. Because we have used Word's standard heading styles (**Heading 1**, **Heading 2** and **Heading 3**) for the different section headings throughout the document, Word can easily use these to build up a table of contents.

 Open **Recipe Book.doc**, switch to **Outline Layout** view and expand the subdocuments.

You can add a table of contents without first expanding the subdocuments (Word will prompt you at the appropriate time), but you may find that it appears in the wrong place!

 Switch to **Print Layout** view and position your insertion point at the end of the **Contents** line. Press **Enter**, so that you create a new blank line under the **Contents** heading, as shown in Figure 5.1. Make sure that the style of the blank line is **Normal**, not **Heading 1**.

·<u>Contents</u>¶

¶···Section Break (Next Page)···

Figure 5.1: Adding a new blank line for the table of contents

Syllabus Ref: AM3.2.2.1
Create a table of contents.

 From the menu, select **Insert, Reference, Index and Tables**. The **Index and Tables** dialogue will be displayed.

 Click the **Table of Contents** tab and set the **Format** to **Formal**, as shown in Figure 5.2. Press **OK** to add the new table of contents.

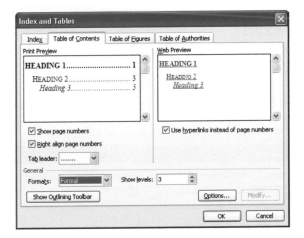

Figure 5.2: Inserting a table of contents

A table of contents should be generated, looking like Figure 5.3.

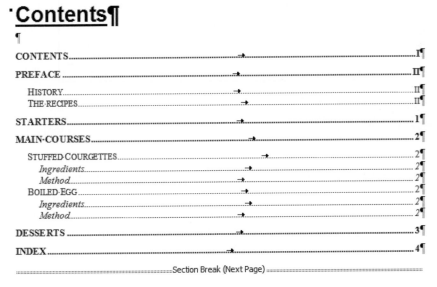

·Contents¶

...............Section Break (Next Page)...............

Figure 5.3: Table of contents generated automatically

This is a reasonable starting point, but notice how the **Ingredients** and **Method** headings are listed for each of the recipes. This is because, by default, a table of contents is generated from three levels of headings in the document, and the **Ingredients** and **Method** headings are in the **Heading 3** style.

Let's regenerate the table of contents using only the first two heading levels.

 Click anywhere in the existing table of contents to select it (it will go grey).

 From the menu, select **Insert**, **Reference**, **Index and Tables** as before.

> ### Syllabus Ref: AM3.2.2.3
> Apply formatting options to a table of contents.

 This time, change **Show levels** down to **2** and change the **Tab leader** to a solid line, as shown in Figure 5.4. Then press **OK**.

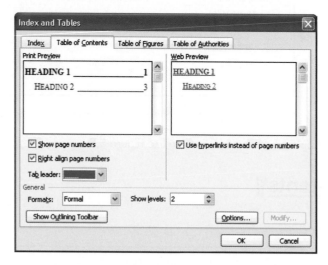

Figure 5.4: Changing the format of a table of contents

 A dialogue will ask you if you want to replace the selected table of contents. You do, so press **OK**.

You can edit the text of a generated table of contents just as you would with any other part of your document, although you might lose these changes when you next update the table of contents (if you choose **Update entire table** rather than **Update page numbers only**).

> ### Syllabus Ref: AM3.2.2.2
> Update and modify an existing table of contents.

Let's try this out. It seems pointless to list the **Contents** page in the table of contents itself, so let's delete it.

 Click in the first line of the table of contents. The easiest way to delete this line is to make sure that the insertion point is **not** at the beginning of the line, then press **Shift+End** (to select the line) and then **Delete** to delete it.

> **TIP**
> If the cursor is at the beginning of the line then **Shift+End** will select the whole table, not just the first line.

The table of contents should now look like Figure 5.5.

`Contents`¶

¶

·····································Section Break (Next Page)·····································

Figure 5.5: Table of contents that has been edited

 With your insertion point somewhere in the table of contents, press the **F9** key; this is the quick way to update a **field** (you'll see on page 89 exactly what this means).
The **Update Table of Contents** dialogue appears.

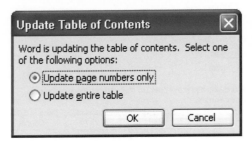

Figure 5.6: Updating the table of contents

The top option would update the page numbers for the headings that are already listed in the table; it would not add the line for **Contents** back in, and it would not find any new recipes that have been added since the table was first generated. The second option would regenerate the entire table (using the same settings, such as using two levels of headings).

 For now, just press **Cancel**, since we know the table of contents is up to date.

Indexes

You can use a similar method to replace the dummy index at the end of the document with a real one. First, you must go through the document marking the keywords. These can then be used to build the index, allowing you to update it automatically after you make changes to the document.

Let's create index entries for the ingredients used in the recipes we have so far.

 Go to the **Main Courses** section and, in the heading **Stuffed Courgettes, double-click** the word **Courgettes** to highlight it.

 Just as for the table of contents, from the menu select **Insert, Reference, Index and Tables**. This time select the **Index** tab.

> **Syllabus Ref: AM3.3.2.2**
>
> Create or edit an index.

Note that we're not creating the index itself yet; we're just using the indexing dialogue to bring up the **Mark Index Entry** dialogue, which we can use to mark the words that should appear in the index when we do generate it.

 Press the **Mark Entry** button to display the **Mark Index Entry** dialogue shown in Figure 5.7.

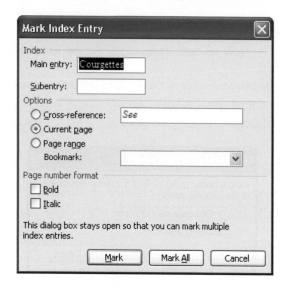

Figure 5.7: Marking a word for inclusion in the index

The **Mark Index Entry** dialogue, unlike many others, lets you carry on working with the document. This is useful because you can leave the dialogue open while you move through the document highlighting all of the terms that you want to appear in the index.

You should decide at this stage whether you want your index entries to start with upper or lower case letters, because the **Main entry** text will be used exactly as it is entered. I recommend using lower case for everything that would be lower case in normal text (so, for example, a person's surname would still start with a capital letter).

 Edit the **Main entry** so that it starts with a lower case **c**.

 Press **Mark**.

You will see some strange text appear in your document, as shown in Figure 5.8. This is a **field code**, which we'll get to later. Don't worry for now – it won't appear on the printed version of the document.

TIP

You can use the **Show/Hide ¶** button on the **Standard** toolbar to toggle the display of these field codes on and off.

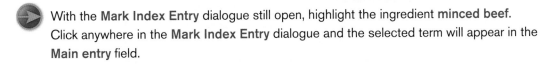

Figure 5.8: A field code marking an index entry (the line happens to be formatted in small caps)

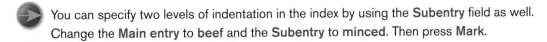 With the **Mark Index Entry** dialogue still open, highlight the ingredient **minced beef**. Click anywhere in the **Mark Index Entry** dialogue and the selected term will appear in the **Main entry** field.

 You can specify two levels of indentation in the index by using the **Subentry** field as well. Change the **Main entry** to **beef** and the **Subentry** to **minced**. Then press **Mark**.

TIP

Notice how the field code for this index entry uses a colon between the two terms.

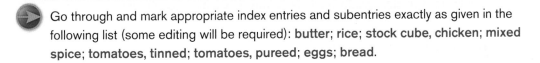 Go through and mark appropriate index entries and subentries exactly as given in the following list (some editing will be required): **butter**; **rice**; **stock cube, chicken**; **mixed spice**; **tomatoes, tinned**; **tomatoes, pureed**; **eggs**; **bread**.

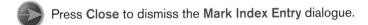 Press **Close** to dismiss the **Mark Index Entry** dialogue.

TIP

Indexes manage their columns without using sections, so our original section break can be deleted.

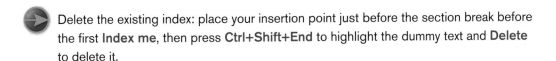 Delete the existing index: place your insertion point just before the section break before the first **Index me**, then press **Ctrl+Shift+End** to highlight the dummy text and **Delete** to delete it.

 From the menu, select **Insert, Reference, Index and Tables**. With the **Index** tab selected, set **Formats** to **Formal** and press **OK**.

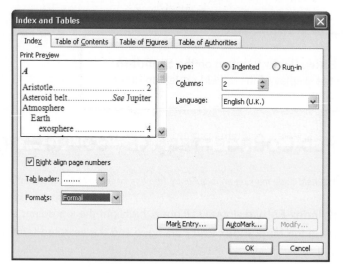

Figure 5.9: Inserting an index

An index will be created, containing the terms you marked (see Figure 5.10). It's not very inspiring yet (everything it refers to is on the same page!), but you can imagine how it will look after the other recipes have been added to the book, and their keywords have been marked too.

You can edit the index by manually changing the text, but any such changes will be lost if you regenerate the index. It is usually better to change the index entry fields as necessary and then refresh the index (which you can update in the same way as a table of contents).

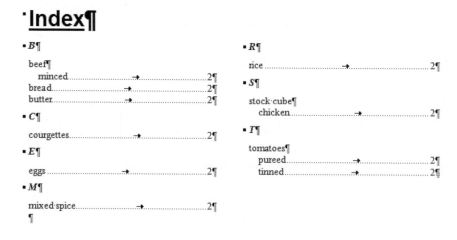

Figure 5.10: Index generated from marked keywords

Bookmarks and cross-references

The index demonstrates how a field can be used to generate a page reference. If you need to refer to a specific item in a document, you can achieve a similar effect by creating a **bookmark** and using a **cross-reference** to it.

Suppose you want to add the following sentence to the preface:

> There are recipes for everyone: page **XXX** even tells you how to boil an egg.

Until the recipe book is finished, you can't put in a fixed value for **XXX** in case it changes. However, if you create a **bookmark** at the location of the boiled egg recipe, you will be able to insert a **cross-reference** to that **bookmark**, which you can refresh with the other **fields** in your document whenever you like.

 Drag your mouse over the entire **boiled egg** recipe to select it.

Syllabus Ref: AM3.3.2.1
Add or delete a bookmark.

From the menu, select **Insert, Bookmark**.

In the **Bookmark** dialogue, type the name **BOILED_EGG** and press **Add**, as shown in Figure 5.11. (Note that this dialogue also has a **Delete** button, which is what you use to remove bookmarks that you no longer need.)

Figure 5.11: Adding a bookmark

> **TIP**
>
> You cannot use spaces in bookmark names. I like to use all capital letters, and to separate words with underscore characters (**Shift+-**).

Bookmark of specific position

Bookmark of a range

Word uses a **grey I-bar** to show the location of a bookmark between characters, and **grey brackets** to show a bookmark that covers a range of text.

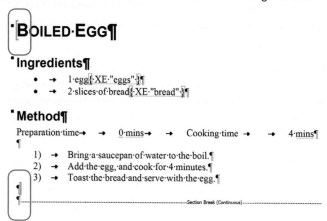

Figure 5.12: Bookmarking a range of text

You can use bookmarks simply for navigating around a document (you don't necessarily have to refer to them from elsewhere). Let's try this.

 Place your insertion point anywhere in the document where you can't see the boiled egg recipe.

 From the menu, select **Edit**, **Go To**. The **Find and Replace** dialogue will be displayed, with the **Go To** tab selected.

 From the **Go to what** list select **Bookmark**. Since **BOILED_EGG** is the only bookmark in the document, this will be set automatically in the list on the right (see Figure 5.13). Press **Go To**.

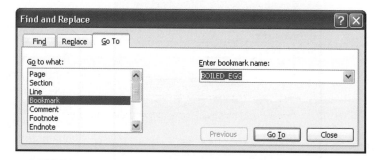

Figure 5.13: Going to a bookmark

The document scrolls to the bookmark. You can use this technique to navigate quickly around any long documents you write.

 Press **Close** to dismiss the **Find and Replace** dialogue.

However, the point of adding this **bookmark** to the document was not to ease navigation, but to allow you to add a **cross-reference** to its page number from the preface.

 Add the following new paragraph between the two existing paragraphs under **The recipes** in the preface:

There are recipes for everyone: page XXX even tells you how to boil an egg.

 Select the **XXX** (not the space after it). We are going to replace this with the **cross-reference**.

 From the menu, select **Insert, Reference, Cross-reference**. The **Cross-reference** dialogue will open.

Syllabus Ref: AM3.3.2.3
Create or delete a cross-reference.

 For the **Reference type**, select **Bookmark**. For **Insert reference to** select **Page number**.
There should be only one entry – **BOILED_EGG** – in the **For which bookmark** list, as shown in Figure 5.14. Press **Insert** and then press **Close**.

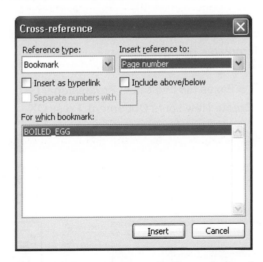

Figure 5.14: Inserting a cross-reference to a bookmark

The paragraph you added should now read as follows:

There are recipes for everyone: page 2 even tells you how to boil an egg.

 Save and close **Recipe Book.doc**.

 TIP
You can delete a cross-reference in the same way as any other field – select it and press the **Delete** key.

'Master Brain' example

Introduction

Tables of contents and indexes are special types of Word objects called **fields**. We are going to create a new document (a letter) that will allow you to learn how to use fields to create powerful, flexible documents.

Imagine that you are a researcher on the quiz show *Master Brain*. The show has been running for ten years and the producer wants you to contact previous contestants to find out if they want to take part in a special anniversary edition of the quiz.

The previous contestants' details are stored in a database, so you just need to produce a form letter that you can send to them (you'll learn how to use **mail merge** to add the addresses to the letters in Chapter 10).

Fields

As an easy way to get the letter started, let's use one of Word's letter templates.

 From the menu, select **File**, **New**. This will open the **New Document** task pane.

 From the **Templates** section in the middle of the task pane, select **On my computer**. This will open the **Templates** dialogue.

 Click on the **Letters & Faxes** tab and select **Professional Letter.dot**, as shown in Figure 5.15. Leave **Create New** set to **Document**. Press **OK**.

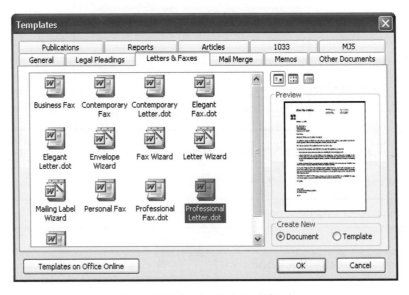

Figure 5.15: Starting the Letter Wizard

You should then get a new blank document like the one shown in Figure 5.16.

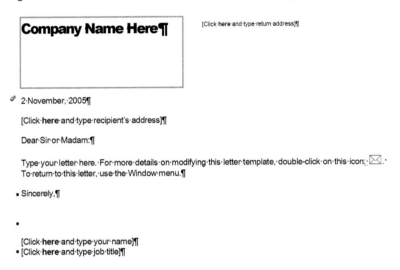

Figure 5.16: Blank letter created from template

There are several **fields** in the document at this stage. The ones that say **Click here** aren't very interesting – they simply allow you to select the whole line when you click on them. Let's look instead at the date.

 Right-click anywhere on the date line (which should have the current date) and select **Toggle field codes** from the menu.

The date should have been replaced with the text **{DATE \@ "d MMMM, yyyy"}**. This shows that this field contains the current date, in the format of day number (**d**), full month name (**MMMM**) and four digit year (**yyyy**).

To show that you can edit the **field code** directly, let's change it to display a two-digit year.

 In the same way that you would edit any other text in a document, delete from the date **field code** two of the four **ys** that represent the year.

 Right-click the date field again and toggle it back so that it displays the date instead of the field code. It will still display in the old format.

 Right-click the date field again and this time choose **Update field**. The date should now display with a two-digit year.

 Edit the rest of the text of the letter so that it looks like Figure 5.17.

Master Brain¶

Master·Brain·10th·Anniversary·Show¶
Unit·7¶
Smartypants·Lane¶
Cleverton¶
BR4·1NY¶

2·November,·05¶

[Click·**here**·and·type·recipient's·address]¶

Dear·Sir·or·Madam:¶

Master· Brain· will· be· ten· years· old· this· spring!· To· celebrate,· we· are· planning· several· special· anniversary· shows·where· previous· contestants·can· again· pit· their· wits· against· the· Memory·Bank· for·a·cash·prize·of·up·to·£1000.¶

If·you·would· like·to·take· part,·or·to·discuss·the·details,·please·contact·me·at·the·address·given·at· the·top·of·this·letter,·giving·your·name·and·a·daytime·contact·telephone·number.·Remember,·you· could·win·£1000!¶

We·look·forward·to·seeing·you·in·the·spring.··Good·luck!¶

· Sincerely,¶

·

Annie·Versary¶
· Researcher¶

Figure 5.17: Creating an invitation for the Master Brain anniversary show

Now, suppose that different shows will have different top prizes: perhaps only the show featuring previous grand champions will have a £1000 top prize, with the others offering only £500.

This letter is so short that it is easy to change both of the references to the prize money as necessary, however you can imagine that for longer, more complicated documents, it could be quite easy for repeated information to get out of sync. We'll use a **field code** to overcome this problem.

> **Syllabus Ref: AM3.3.3.1**
> Insert a field code.

 From the menu, select **File**, **Properties** and select the **Custom** tab.

In the **Name** box type **Top prize**, and enter a **Value** of **£1000** (see Figure 5.18). Then click **Add**, followed by **OK**.

Figure 5.18: Adding a new property to a document

 Select the first occurrence of **£1000** in the letter. From the menu, choose **Insert**, **Field**.

In the **Field** dialogue, select a **Field name** of **DocProperty** and a **Property** of **Top prize**, as shown in Figure 5.19. Press **OK**.

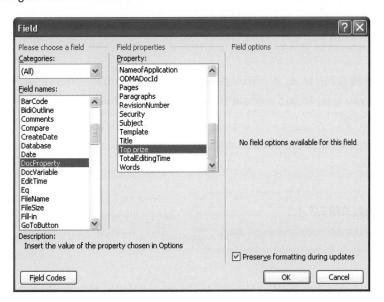

Figure 5.19: Adding a field to the document

When the dialogue closes, it doesn't look like anything has changed. However, if you click on the first **£1000** you will see the telltale grey box that shows it is a field rather than just plain text. If you're feeling curious, toggle the field code on and then off again.

Highlight the second **£1000** and change this to another field referring to the document property.

The benefit of adding the fields is that it is now easy to change the top prize.

 From the menu, select **File, Properties**.

 With the **Custom** tab displayed, click on the **Top prize** line in the **Properties** list. Change the **Value** to **£500** and click **Modify** (which has replaced **Add**). Finally, click **OK**.

To see the change, you have to update the fields in the document.

 From the menu, choose **Edit, Select All**. Then **right-click** and select **Update Field**.

Both of the references to prize money should now say **£500** instead of **£1000**.

> **Syllabus Ref: AM3.3.3.4**
> Delete a field code.

It is slightly more complicated to delete a field than it is to delete normal text. **Don't delete any fields for now**, but you need to know the method: place your insertion point immediately to the left of the field, which will highlight the field in light grey; press **Delete**, which will highlight the field in dark grey, but nothing will be deleted yet; to actually delete the field, press **Delete** again.

Footnotes

The final thing we're going to do in this chapter is to add a **footnote** to the letter. Footnotes are often used when you want to add an explanation that would distract the reader if it was just put in the main text.

We'll add a footnote to explain that not every contestant who responds to the letter is guaranteed a place in the show.

> **Syllabus Ref: AM3.3.4.1**
> Create or delete footnotes and endnotes.

 Position your insertion point at the end of the phrase **If you would like to take part** (before the comma).

 From the menu, select **Insert, Reference, Footnote**.

The **Footnote and Endnote** dialogue is displayed. Change the fields to match those shown in Figure 5.20 (if they do not already match): these specify that you want to add a numbered footnote at the bottom of the page. Press **Insert**.

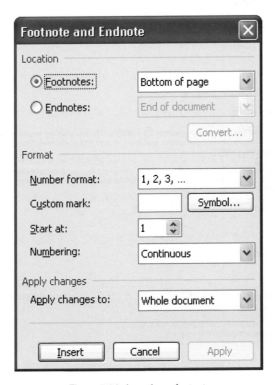

Figure 5.20: Inserting a footnote

Word will scroll to the bottom of the page, with the insertion point positioned after a superscript number one.

 Type **Not all respondents are guaranteed a place.**

Let's add another footnote, before the first, to see what happens.

 Place your insertion point after the first £500 (before the full stop) and insert another numbered footnote. This time type **Maximum prize is subject to change without notice.**

The finished document should look like Figure 5.21 (in which the document is shown using a split window, so you can see the top and bottom together).

Figure 5.21: Document including footnotes (shown in a split window)

Notice how, if you hover your mouse pointer over a footnote field in the document body (that is, one of the superscript numbers), Word pops up a box showing the footnote text (see Figure 5.22).

Figure 5.22: Pop-up showing the text of a footnote

Syllabus Ref: AM3.3.4.2

Modify existing footnotes or endnotes.

You can edit footnotes after you have created them: just click on their text and type as you normally would. You can modify their formatting, for example by making certain words bold, just as with any other text.

Change the first footnote to read **All prizes are** instead of **Maximum prize is**, and underline **without notice**.

Syllabus Ref: AM3.3.4.3
Modify format and positioning of
footnotes or endnotes.

You can also move footnote references around in the text, as follows.

 Select the footnote field for the first footnote (the superscript 1 after the **£500**). From the menu, select **Edit, Cut.**

Notice how the associated footnote disappears from the bottom of the page and the other footnote is renumbered from **2** to **1**.

 Position your insertion point between the second **£500** and the exclamation mark that follows it. From the menu, select **Edit, Paste.**

The footnote has been added back in to the document and has been renumbered as it now comes after the other footnote.

Endnotes are treated exactly like **footnotes**, except that they appear at the very end of the document (or section) regardless of which page they are referenced from; you create them in the same way, but select **Endnotes** instead of **Footnotes** in the dialogue. You can click on the text to edit it, and you can delete an **endnote** (or **footnote**, or any other **field**) by selecting the **field reference** and pressing the **Delete** key.

 Save the document as **Master Brain.doc.**

Test yourself

1. Experiment with adding page ranges to an index, using a new blank document. The method is as follows: (1) select a range of text that covers two or more pages, (2) create a bookmark for the selected text, (3) add an index entry referencing the bookmark, (4) generate the index as usual.

2. It would be better if we could regenerate the table of contents for the recipe book without having to manually delete the 'Contents' entry. Create a new paragraph style called **Heading 1 No Contents** based on **Heading 1** and set the 'Contents' heading to use this new style. Use the **Options** button from the **Index and Tables** dialogue to delete the **TOC level** next to the new style (make sure you delete the **TOC level** number, rather than setting it to **0**). Regenerate the table of contents to check that the line for 'Contents' does not appear.

3. In a blank document, type the text **Written by [Author]**, where **[Author]** is an inserted **Author** field. Select this text and use it to create a new **AutoText** entry. Confirm that now when you start to type **Written by** you can press **Enter** to have **Written by [Your Name]** inserted automatically. Notice how the name is still a field (it goes grey when you click it).

6 Tables

Introduction

In this chapter, we will look at how to create tables in Word. As an example, you will create a table that lists the top ten best-selling albums of all time in the USA. You probably already know how to create simple tables in Word, but this example will cover some more advanced subjects.

In this chapter you will

    use **text orientation options** to make headings fit more neatly into a tight space

    see why it can be useful to **split** or **merge** cells, and how to do this

    learn how to **convert tabbed text to a table**, and a table back to text

    see how to **sort** the contents of a table

    find out how Word can automatically **sum** the numbers in a table

    see why Word's built-in **captions** are a more powerful solution than just manually typing caption text after an object.

Top 10 albums

So that we have some real information to work with for this chapter, we will be developing a table that lists the top 10 albums of all time (based on USA sales):

Rank	Artist	Title	Label	Sales (m)
1	The Eagles	Eagles/Their Greatest Hits 1971–1975	Elektra	28
2	Michael Jackson	Thriller	Epic	26
3	Pink Floyd	The Wall	Columbia	23
4	Led Zeppelin	Led Zeppelin IV	Swan Song	22
5	Billy Joel	Greatest Hits Volume I & Volume II	Columbia	21
6	Fleetwood Mac	Rumours	Warner Bros.	19
7	AC/DC	Back in Black	Elektra	19
8	The Beatles	The Beatles	Capitol	19
9	Shania Twain	Come on Over	Mercury Nashville	19
10	Boston	Boston	Epic	17

Figure 6.1: Top 10 best-selling albums of all time (USA). Data provided by the Recording Industry Association of America.

To start with, let's create a new document and put this information in a simple table. Then we can start to play with the interesting stuff.

 Create a new blank document. Add a level 1 heading **Music Sales** and a level 2 heading **Top 10 Albums**.

 Place your insertion point on the line beneath the **Top 10 Albums** line and from the menu select **Table, Insert, Table**.

 Set the **Number of columns** to **6** and the **Number of rows** to **11**, as shown in Figure 6.2. (We're creating an extra column to use later.) Press **OK**.

Figure 6.2: Inserting a new table

 Type in the album sales data, as it is given in Figure 6.1.

 Click in the margin to the left of the top (heading) row of the table, which will select that row. Make this heading text bold.

Your initial document should look like Figure 6.3.

˙Music·Sales¶

˙Top·10·Albums¶

Rank¤	Artist¤	Title¤	Label¤	Sales·(m)¤	¤	¤
1¤	The·Eagles¤	Eagles/Their· Greatest·Hits· 1971–1975¤	Elektra¤	28¤	¤	¤
2¤	Michael· Jackson¤	Thriller¤	Epic¤	26¤	¤	¤
3¤	Pink·Floyd¤	The·Wall¤	Columbia¤	23¤	¤	¤
4¤	Led·Zeppelin¤	Led·Zeppelin· IV¤	Swan·Song¤	22¤	¤	¤
5¤	Billy·Joel¤	Greatest·Hits· Volume·I·&· Volume·II¤	Columbia¤	21¤	¤	¤
6¤	Fleetwood· Mac¤	Rumours¤	Warner·Bros.¤	19¤	¤	¤
7¤	AC/DC¤	Back·in·Black¤	Elektra¤	19¤	¤	¤
8¤	The·Beatles¤	The·Beatles¤	Capitol¤	19¤	¤	¤
9¤	Shania·Twain¤	Come·on·Over¤	Mercury· Nashville¤	19¤	¤	¤
10¤	Boston¤	Boston¤	Epic¤	17¤	¤	¤

¶

Figure 6.3: Simple table with bold headings

Remember you can use the **Tab** key to move between table cells.

Sorting

Once information is in a table, it is straightforward to manipulate it in Word. Suppose we wanted to change the order of the rows, so that the table was sorted alphabetically by label and in reverse alphabetical order by artist within each label (not very likely, I admit!). Let's try it.

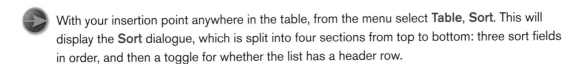

Syllabus Ref: AM3.4.1.3

Sort data (alphabetic or numeric) in a table (ascending or descending order).

With your insertion point anywhere in the table, from the menu select **Table, Sort**. This will display the **Sort** dialogue, which is split into four sections from top to bottom: three sort fields in order, and then a toggle for whether the list has a header row.

Choose to **Sort by** the **Label** column and **Then by** the **Artist** column. Make sure that the second sort field is set to **Descending** (so it is sorted in reverse order) and that the **My list has** area shows **Header row** selected (see Figure 6.4). Then press **OK**.

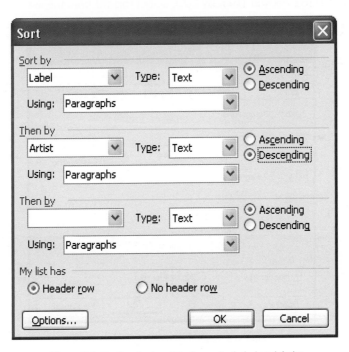

Figure 6.4: Sorting the top 10 albums by Label and Artist

The new sort order should be as shown in Figure 6.5.

˙Music·Sales¶

˙*Top·10·Albums*¶

Rank¤	Artist¤	Title¤	Label¤	Sales·(m)¤	¤
8¤	The·Beatles¤	The·Beatles¤	Capitol¤	19¤	¤
3¤	Pink·Floyd¤	The·Wall¤	Columbia¤	23¤	¤
5¤	Billy·Joel¤	Greatest·Hits·Volume·I·&·Volume·II¤	Columbia¤	21¤	¤
1¤	The·Eagles¤	Eagles/Their·Greatest·Hits·1971–1975¤	Elektra¤	28¤	¤
7¤	AC/DC¤	Back·in·Black¤	Elektra¤	19¤	¤
2¤	Michael·Jackson¤	Thriller¤	Epic¤	26¤	¤
10¤	Boston¤	Boston¤	Epic¤	17¤	¤
9¤	Shania·Twain¤	Come·on·Over¤	Mercury·Nashville¤	19¤	¤
4¤	Led·Zeppelin¤	Led·Zeppelin·IV¤	Swan·Song¤	22¤	¤
6¤	Fleetwood·Mac¤	Rumours¤	Warner·Bros.¤	19¤	¤

Figure 6.5: Top 10 albums after changing the sort order

 Change the sort order back by sorting the table by **Rank** in **Ascending** order (see Figure 6.6). To clear the **Then by** field, select **(none)** from the list. Press **OK** to confirm the new sort order.

Figure 6.6: Returning to sorting by sales rank

Notice that Word has automatically detected that the **Rank** column contains numbers, so has defaulted the field **Type** to **Number** instead of **Text**. If you were to sort the **Rank** as **Text** instead, you would get alphabetical order: 1, 10, 2, 3, 4, 5, 6, 7, 8, 9.

Splitting and merging cells

Sometimes it's useful to be able to split or merge cells, as shown in Figure 6.7. Through a combination of merging and splitting cells, you can produce very complicated table layouts.

	Two cells merged horizontally		
Two cells merged vertically			
	One	cell	
	split	2x2	
	2 cells	merged	then split

Figure 6.7: Examples of split and merged cells (grey cells are unchanged) in a grid with three columns and five rows

Let's try out some merging and splitting on our table of album sales, by renaming the **Title** column **Full Title** and splitting up its contents into **Title** and **Subtitle**.

> **Syllabus Ref: AM3.4.1.1**
> Use merge and split cell options in a table.

 Rename the heading **Title** to **Full Title**.

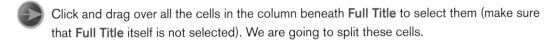 Click and drag over all the cells in the column beneath **Full Title** to select them (make sure that **Full Title** itself is not selected). We are going to split these cells.

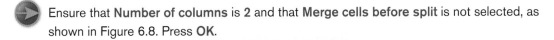 From the menu, select **Table**, **Split Cells**. The **Split Cells** dialogue will appear.

Ensure that **Number of columns** is **2** and that **Merge cells before split** is not selected, as shown in Figure 6.8. Press **OK**.

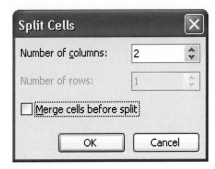

Figure 6.8: Splitting table cells into two columns

Your table should now look like Figure 6.9.

Rank¤	Artist¤	Full·Title¤		Label¤	Sales·(m)¤	¤
1¤	The·Eagles¤	Eagles/Their·Greatest·Hits·1971–1975¤	¤	Elektra¤	28¤	¤
2¤	Michael·Jackson¤	Thriller¤	¤	Epic¤	26¤	¤
3¤	Pink·Floyd¤	The·Wall¤	¤	Columbia¤	23¤	¤
4¤	Led·Zeppelin¤	Led·Zeppelin·IV¤	¤	Swan·Song¤	22¤	¤
5¤	Billy·Joel¤	Greatest·Hits·Volume·I·&·Volume·II¤	¤	Columbia¤	21¤	¤
6¤	Fleetwood·Mac¤	Rumours¤	¤	Warner·Bros.¤	19¤	¤
7¤	AC/DC¤	Back·in·Black¤	¤	Elektra¤	19¤	¤
8¤	The·Beatles¤	The·Beatles¤	¤	Capitol¤	19¤	¤
9¤	Shania·Twain¤	Come·on·Over¤	¤	Mercury·Nashville¤	19¤	¤
10¤	Boston¤	Boston¤	¤	Epic¤	17¤	¤

Figure 6.9: Table with split titles

 Click in the margin to the left of the first album row (**The Eagles**) to select it, then right-click and from that menu select **Insert Rows**. A new blank line is added under the headings.

 In the two blank cells under **Full Title**, enter the headings **Title** and **Subtitle**. Make these cells bold (to match the main title row).

 Select the title cell **Rank** and the blank cell below it. Right-click and from the menu that appears select **Merge Cells**. Repeat this merging for **Artist**, **Label**, and **Sales (m)** and their respective blank cells.

 Finally, split out the subtitles from the two 'Greatest Hits' albums using cut and paste, so that your table looks like Figure 6.10.

Rank¤	Artist¤	Full·Title¤		Label¤	Sales·(m)¤	¤
		Title¤	Subtitle¤			¤
1¤	The·Eagles¤	Eagles¤	Their·Greatest·Hits·1971–1975¤	Elektra¤	28¤	¤
2¤	Michael·Jackson¤	Thriller¤	¤	Epic¤	26¤	¤
3¤	Pink·Floyd¤	The·Wall¤	¤	Columbia¤	23¤	¤
4¤	Led·Zeppelin¤	Led·Zeppelin·IV¤	¤	Swan·Song¤	22¤	¤
5¤	Billy·Joel¤	Greatest·Hits¤	Volume·I·&·Volume·II¤	Columbia¤	21¤	¤
6¤	Fleetwood·Mac¤	Rumours¤	¤	Warner·Bros.¤	19¤	¤
7¤	AC/DC¤	Back·in·Black¤	¤	Elektra¤	19¤	¤
8¤	The·Beatles¤	The·Beatles¤	¤	Capitol¤	19¤	¤
9¤	Shania·Twain¤	Come·on·Over¤	¤	Mercury·Nashville¤	19¤	¤
10¤	Boston¤	Boston¤	¤	Epic¤	17¤	¤

Figure 6.10: Split and merged header cells

Text orientation

Syllabus Ref: AM3.1.1.7

Use text orientation options.

When you are trying to fit a lot of information into a table, it is sometimes useful to change the direction of the text. Often this is used to turn table headings on their sides so that they are written from top to bottom (instead of left to right), particularly when the headings are much longer than the other cells in that column (for example, for columns that contain only ticks or crosses, but have a long name).

We'll use this technique to add some text running down the right-hand side of the table to cite the source of the information it contains.

TIP

This section explains how to change the text orientation for a table cell. You can also change the orientation of text boxes (see Chapter 8, page 145).

 Select all but the top two cells of the blank column on the right of the table by clicking and dragging down them.

Right-click and from this menu select **Merge Cells**. There should now be one large cell the same height as the body of the table, with two cells above it.

Right-click on the large cell and from this menu select **Text Direction**. A dialogue entitled **Text Direction – Table Cell** will appear.

Click on the **Orientation** option that will make the text run down the page (that is, so you can read it if you tilt your head to the right – see Figure 6.11). Press **OK**.

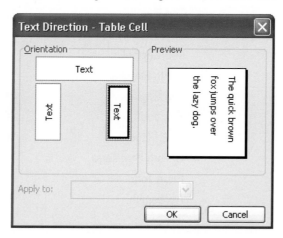

Figure 6.11: Changing the direction of text in a table cell

Notice how the insertion point has tilted on its side (see Figure 6.12). When you start to type in this cell, the text will go from top to bottom.

 Type **Data provided by the Recording Industry Association of America.**

Your table should look like Figure 6.12.

Rank¤	Artist¤	Full·Title¤		Label¤	Sales·(m)¤	¤	
		Title¤	Subtitle¤			¤	
1¤	The·Eagles¤	Eagles¤	Their·Greatest·Hits·1971–1975¤	Elektra¤	28¤		
2¤	Michael·Jackson¤	Thriller¤	¤	Epic¤	26¤		
3¤	Pink·Floyd¤	The·Wall¤	¤	Columbia¤	23¤		
4¤	Led·Zeppelin¤	Led·Zeppelin·IV¤	¤	Swan·Song¤	22¤		
5¤	Billy·Joel¤	Greatest·Hits¤	Volume·I·&·Volume·II¤	Columbia¤	21¤		
6¤	Fleetwood·Mac¤	Rumours¤	¤	Warner·Bros.¤	19¤		
7¤	AC/DC¤	Back·in·Black¤	¤	Elektra¤	19¤		
8¤	The·Beatles¤	The·Beatles¤	¤	Capitol¤	19¤		
9¤	Shania·Twain¤	Come·on·Over¤	¤	Mercury·Nashville¤	19¤		
10¤	Boston¤	Boston¤	¤	Epic¤	17¤		

Data provided by the Recording Industry Association of America¤

Figure 6.12: Rotated text in a table cell

That's it for the content of the table. It looks a bit messy at the moment, but you'll see at the end of this chapter, page 110, that there are some quick ways to smarten it up.

First, we're going to add a second table to the document.

Top 10 artists

We're going to create a second table in the document, to look at some more of Word's features. To continue the previous example, we will use a list of the top 10 best-selling artists of all time.

Rank	Artist	Certified Units (m)
1	The Beatles	166.5
2	Elvis Presley	117.5
3	Led Zeppelin	106.0
4	Garth Brooks	105.0
5	The Eagles	88.0
6	Billy Joel	78.5
7	Pink Floyd	73.5
8	Barbra Streisand	71.5
9	Elton John	67.5
10	Aerosmith	64.0

Figure 6.13: Top 10 best-selling artists in the USA, based on album sales. Data provided by the Recording Industry Association of America.

Sometimes you will already have some information in text form that you want to turn into a table in Word. This is easy to do, as the following example will show.

 Press **Enter** once or twice below the **Top 10 Albums** table to create some blank lines. With a gap below the existing table, enter the title **Top 10 Artists** in the **Heading 2** style.

 Below the new heading, type the contents of Figure 6.13 (including the headings) just as text; press **Tab** between each rank, artist and sales figure, and press **Enter** at the end of each line.

Top·10·Artists¶

Rank	Artist	Certified·Units·(m)¶
1	The·Beatles	166.5¶
2	Elvis·Presley	117.5¶
3	Led·Zeppelin	106.0¶
4	Garth·Brooks	105.0¶
5	The·Eagles	88.0¶
6	Billy·Joel	78.5¶
7	Pink·Floyd	73.5¶
8	Barbra·Streisand	71.5¶
9	Elton·John	67.5¶
10	Aerosmith	64.0¶

Figure 6.14: Entering a table as tabbed text

> **Syllabus Ref: AM3.4.1.2**
> Convert tabbed text into a table.

 Select all of the text for the new table (everything below **Top 10 Artists**) and from the menu choose **Table, Convert, Text to Table**.

 The **Convert Text to Table** dialogue appears. It should automatically detect that there are three columns separated by tabs, so it should look like Figure 6.15. Press **OK**.

Figure 6.15: Converting tabbed text to a three-column table

You should now have a three-column table. Note that there is a similar option (**Table, Convert, Table to Text**) for converting back in the other direction.

Automatic sums

Suppose you wanted to put the total album sales of the top ten artists combined at the bottom of the table. You could work this out yourself or you could get Word to do the calculation manually: this second option is useful if you want the total to update automatically whenever the values in the table are changed.

> **Syllabus Ref: AM3.4.1.4**
> Perform addition calculations on a numeric list in a table.

 Put your insertion point in the last cell in the table (**64.0**) and press **Tab**. This is the quickest way to add a new row to the end.

 Press **Tab** twice more so that your insertion point is in the cell below all the numbers.

 From the menu, select **Table, Formula**. The **Formula** dialogue appears.

 The **Formula** is automatically set to **=SUM(ABOVE)** because Word detects that you are inserting the formula at the bottom of a column of numbers. This is exactly what we want! (If you insert a formula in the last cell of a row of numbers, the **Formula** defaults to **=SUM(LEFT)** instead.) For the **Number format** type **0.0**, which tells Word to use exactly one decimal place – this will look neater in this example, since all of the other numbers use one decimal place, but you won't need to remember this for the exam (although you should be aware of the other formats given in the drop-down list). Press **OK**.

Figure 6.16: Inserting a formula into a table cell

The total **938.0** should appear in the cell, as shown in Figure 6.17.

Top·10·Artists¶

Rank¤	Artist¤	Certified·Units·(m)¤
1¤	The·Beatles¤	166.5¤
2¤	Elvis·Presley¤	117.5¤
3¤	Led·Zeppelin¤	106.0¤
4¤	Garth·Brooks¤	105.0¤
5¤	The·Eagles¤	88.0¤
6¤	Billy·Joel¤	78.5¤
7¤	Pink·Floyd¤	73.5¤
8¤	Barbra·Streisand¤	71.5¤
9¤	Elton·John¤	67.5¤
10¤	Aerosmith¤	64.0¤
¤	¤	938.0¤

Figure 6.17: A table with a formula summing the contents of a column

Captions

Syllabus Ref: AM3.4.6.1

Add or update a caption to an image, table.

Syllabus Ref: AM3.4.6.2

Apply a numbered caption to an image, figures, table or worksheet.

Let's add a **caption** to each of our tables. A **caption** is a numbered description associated with some object in a document: a table, a figure, an image, a worksheet or an equation. The same procedure is used for each (although captions are traditionally placed above tables but below images), but we'll look at adding captions to tables.

Place your insertion point anywhere in the **Top 10 Albums** table and from the menu select **Insert, Reference, Caption**. The **Caption** dialogue appears.

Make sure that **Label** is set to **Table**, that **Position** is **Above selected item** and that **Exclude label from caption** is not ticked. The **Caption** should automatically be set to **Table 1** (if it says something else, go into **Numbering** and untick **Include chapter number**). Press **OK**.

Figure 6.18: Inserting a table caption

The text **Table 1** should have been added just above the table.

TIP

Once you have added a caption, you can edit it just like any other text in your document.

 After the text **Table 1**, type **: Biggest-selling albums of all time in the USA.**

 Add a similar caption to the second table, so that it ends up reading **Table 2: Biggest-selling artists of all time in the USA, based on album sales.**

Syllabus Ref: AM3.4.6.3
Use automatic caption options.

Rather than manually adding a caption each time you add a particular type of object, you could instead use **AutoCaption**. If you press the **AutoCaption** button from the **Caption** dialogue, you get the **AutoCaption** dialogue, as shown in Figure 6.19 (which shows the option selected to automatically add a caption to each table you create).

You may be asked to use **AutoCaption** in the ECDL exam, so you need to remember how to turn it on or off. However, for the purposes of this exercise, do not turn on **AutoCaption** for any object types.

Figure 6.19: Setting the option to automatically add a caption to each new table

The biggest benefit of using captions, rather than just typing the numbers by hand, comes if you decide to rearrange the order of things in your document.

 Select everything connected with the second table: the title **Top 10 Artists**, the caption, and the table itself.

 Click on any of the selected text and, keeping your mouse button down, drag it up the document. Your pointer will change so that it has a **grey rectangle** attached to it (see Figure 6.20, which shows the drag in progress) and the **text insertion point** will move with it. Release the mouse button only when the **text insertion point** is on the left of the title **Top 10 Albums.**

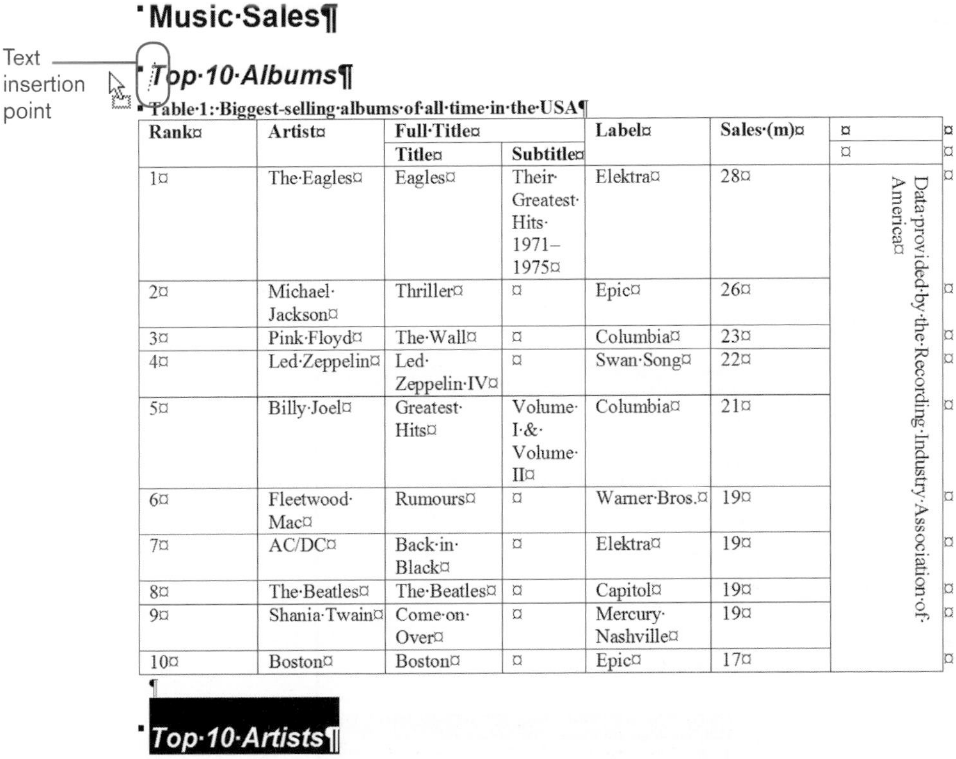

Music Sales

Text insertion point

Top 10 Albums

Table 1: Biggest-selling albums of all time in the USA

Rank	Artist	Full Title		Label	Sales (m)		Data provided by the Recording Industry Association of America
		Title	Subtitle				
1	The Eagles	Eagles	Their Greatest Hits 1971–1975	Elektra	28		
2	Michael Jackson	Thriller		Epic	26		
3	Pink Floyd	The Wall		Columbia	23		
4	Led Zeppelin	Led Zeppelin IV		Swan Song	22		
5	Billy Joel	Greatest Hits	Volume I & Volume II	Columbia	21		
6	Fleetwood Mac	Rumours		Warner Bros.	19		
7	AC/DC	Back in Black		Elektra	19		
8	The Beatles	The Beatles		Capitol	19		
9	Shania Twain	Come on Over		Mercury Nashville	19		
10	Boston	Boston		Epic	17		

Top 10 Artists

Figure 6.20: Moving selected text using 'drag and drop'. This shows the drag in progress, not the final order.

This is a useful technique for moving any text around your document, not just tables.

You should now have **Top 10 Artists** before **Top 10 Albums** in your document, although the captions will now be in the wrong order: **Table 2** coming before **Table 1**. However, refreshing the document's **fields** will fix this.

From the menu, choose **Edit**, **Select All**.

Right-click anywhere in the document and from this menu select **Update Field**.

This updates all of the fields in the document; in particular, **Table 1** now comes before **Table 2**. Had you had any **cross-references** to tables, these would also have been kept in sync with the changed order.

Table AutoFormat

This last section isn't part of the ECDL syllabus, so you can skip it if you like. However, it does show how you can use Word to smarten up your tables with very little effort on your part.

 With your text insertion point anywhere in the second table, from the menu select **Table**, **Table AutoFormat**.

 Select **Table Classic 3** from the list of **Table styles**. Make sure that **Apply special formats to** has only **Heading rows** ticked, as shown in Figure 6.21. Press **Apply**.

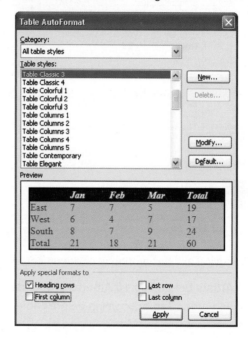

Figure 6.21: Automatically formatting a table

This goes some way to improving the look of the table, but there are still some things to improve: Word hasn't worked out that **Title** and **Subtitle** are part of the heading row, so they have the wrong format and there is too much wasted space in the table.

 Select the **Full Title** and **Title** cells and from the menu select **Table**, **Heading Rows Repeat**. This flags the top two rows as headings and would repeat them at the top of each page if the table ran across a page boundary.

Normally, you would select the whole row for each of the rows you want to set as a heading. However, this is very tricky with the mouse when you have merged cells; selecting the cells works just as well.

Select the two blank cells in the top-right corner. Right-click and from this menu select **Delete Cells**. The **Delete Cells** dialogue is displayed, as shown in Figure 6.22.

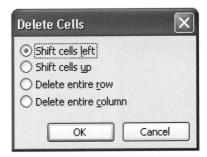

Figure 6.22: Deleting table cells

 Make sure that **Shift cells left** is selected and press **OK**. In this case there are no cells to the right, so this option will simply 'cut out' the top-right corner of the table.

 From the menu select **Table, AutoFit, AutoFit to Contents**.

Word changes the column widths to fit the contents – the table looks a lot better spaced out than it did before.

 You'll find that Word has been a bit miserly with the width of the rightmost column, so that half of the bottom line of rotated text has been cut off. The quick way to fix this is to **double-click** the right-hand border of the table, which resizes it to fit.

The table headings will look better centred.

 Click to the left of the headings to select the top row, and then press the **Center** button on the **Formatting** toolbar. Click in the **Title** and **Subtitle** cells in turn, centring each.

Center

Apply the same type of formatting to the top table: apply the **AutoFormat** style **Table Classic 3** (this time with special formatting applied to both the heading and last rows), **AutoFit to Contents**, and centre the headings.

Select all of the cells containing numbers (click and drag down the **Rank** numbers, then hold down the **Ctrl** key and click and drag down the **Certified Units** numbers) and then press the **Align Right** button on the **Formatting** toolbar.

Align Right

The final document should look like Figure 6.23.

 Save the document as **Music Sales.doc**.

˙**Music·Sales¶**

˙*Top·10·Artists¶*

▪ Table·1:·Biggest-selling·artists·of·all·time·in·the·USA,·based·on·album·sales¶

Rank¤	*Artist*¤	*Certified·Units·(m)*¤	¤
1¤	The·Beatles¤	166.5¤	¤
2¤	Elvis·Presley¤	117.5¤	¤
3¤	Led·Zeppelin¤	106.0¤	¤
4¤	Garth·Brooks¤	105.0¤	¤
5¤	The·Eagles¤	88.0¤	¤
6¤	Billy·Joel¤	78.5¤	¤
7¤	Pink·Floyd¤	73.5¤	¤
8¤	Barbra·Streisand¤	71.5¤	¤
9¤	Elton·John¤	67.5¤	¤
10¤	Aerosmith¤	64.0¤	¤
¤	¤	938.0¤	¤

˙*Top·10·Albums¶*

▪ Table·2:·Biggest-selling·albums·of·all·time·in·the·USA¶

Rank¤	*Artist*¤	*Full·Title*¤		*Label*¤	*Sales·*	¤
		Title¤	*Subtitle*¤		*(m)*¤	¤
1¤	The·Eagles¤	Eagles¤	Their·Greatest·Hits· 1971–1975¤	Elektra¤	28¤	¤
2¤	Michael· Jackson¤	Thriller¤	¤	Epic¤	26¤	¤
3¤	Pink·Floyd¤	The·Wall¤	¤	Columbia¤	23¤	¤
4¤	Led·Zeppelin¤	Led·Zeppelin· IV¤	¤	Swan·Song¤	22¤	¤
5¤	Billy·Joel¤	Greatest·Hits¤	Volume·I·&·Volume·II¤	Columbia¤	21¤	¤
6¤	Fleetwood· Mac¤	Rumours¤	¤	Warner·Bros.¤	19¤	¤
7¤	AC/DC¤	Back·in·Black¤	¤	Elektra¤	19¤	¤
8¤	The·Beatles¤	The·Beatles¤	¤	Capitol¤	19¤	¤
9¤	Shania·Twain¤	Come·on· Over¤	¤	Mercury· Nashville¤	19¤	¤
10¤	Boston¤	Boston¤	¤	Epic¤	17¤	¤

Data·provided·by·the·Recording· Industry·Association·of·America¤

Figure 6.23: Table with AutoFormat and AutoFit applied

Test yourself

1. Try drawing a table using the **Table, Draw Table** menu option. Also try using this tool to split some cells.

2. Set up **AutoCaption** so that you automatically get a caption created each time you add a new table. After trying it out, you may want to turn the option off again.

3. Create a table with 15 rows and 15 columns, and turn it into a crossword puzzle. Use superscript formatting for the numbers in any cells that are at the start of a word. Use hidden text for the letters that form the answers, so that they disappear when you toggle off viewing hidden text. Put the clues in their own section, with two columns (one each for Across and Down clues) below the puzzle. Fill any blank cells with black.

7 Sharing Documents

Introduction

In this chapter, we will look at the features that Word provides to help you to share documents with other people.

We will create a food order form for a staff Christmas party. People would receive the form by email and make their food choices in Word. They could then email or print their completed forms.

We will also look at how Word might be used to review and revise the Master Brain letter we created in Chapter 5.

In this chapter you will

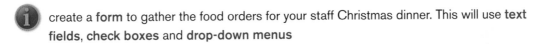 create a **form** to gather the food orders for your staff Christmas dinner. This will use **text fields**, **check boxes** and **drop-down menus**

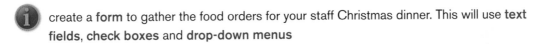 see how to add **comments** to the Master Brain letter, flagging up queries or things to remember for later

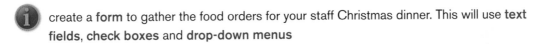 learn how to **track changes** made to a document and how to **accept** or **reject** those changes

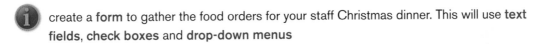 add a **password** to the document, so that people who do not know the password cannot open it.

Forms

Syllabus Ref: AM3.4.2.1
Create and edit a form.

A form is often the best way of collecting information. As well as allowing you to create forms that can be printed out and written on, Word has some special features for dealing with forms that can be filled in from within Word itself. We're going to look at this by creating an example form, asking staff to select the courses for their Christmas dinner and to say when they are available.

Word has a special toolbar dedicated to forms, so let's start by making sure that this is displayed.

 From the menu, select **View**, **Toolbars** and tick **Forms** if it is not already ticked. This will display the **Forms** toolbar, as shown in Figure 7.1.

Figure 7.1: The Forms toolbar

The buttons are as follows:

abl	**Text Form Field**	▦	**Insert Table**
☑	**Check Box Form Field**	▦	**Insert Frame**
▤	**Drop-Down Form Field**	a	**Form Field Shading**
☞	**Form Field Options**	✐	**Reset Form Fields**
✎	**Draw Table**	🔒	**Protect/Unprotect Form**

 Open a new document and type the title **Christmas Dinner Orders** in the **Heading 1** style.

 On the blank line after the heading, set the font size to **14** and type the introductory text shown in Figure 7.2.

˙Christmas·Dinner·Orders¶

This·year's·Christmas·Dinner·will·be·at·the·Plough·and·Furrow·on·the·5ᵗʰ,· 6ᵗʰ·or·7ᵗʰ·of·December·(whichever·day·most·people·can·make).¶

¶

Please·fill·in·the·following·form·with·your·food·preferences,·and·return·it· to·me·by·the·end·of·this·week.¶

¶

Figure 7.2: Introductory text for the Christmas dinner order form

After this text, insert a table to hold the form fields; this will make sure that they line up tidily.

 Click the **Insert Table** button on the **Forms** toolbar and drag out over a 5 x 2 area before releasing the mouse button, as shown in Figure 7.3.

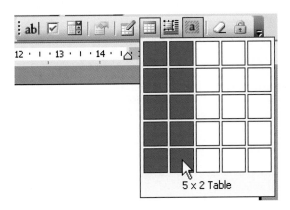

Figure 7.3: Inserting a 5 x 2 table to hold the form

 In the first column enter the titles **Name:**, **Starter:**, **Main Course:**, **Dessert:** and **Dates Available:**.

The form you now have would do the job: you could print it out and ask people to write in their choices. However, you would have no control over what they could write: someone may try to order beans on toast for their main course, even though this isn't on the Plough and Furrow's Christmas menu.

The benefit of using Word forms is that they give you control over the information that can be entered.

> **Syllabus Ref: AM3.4.2.2**
> Use available form field options: text field, check box, drop-down menu etc.

 Click in the top cell of the right-hand column, which is where we want the recipient to enter their name. Press the **Text Form Field** button on the **Forms** toolbar. A grey rectangle appears.

Text Form Field

 Double-click the new form field (grey rectangle). The **Text Form Field Options** dialogue appears.

The default **Maximum length** is **unlimited**. Change this to the more realistic limit of **30**. Also, because this is a name, set the **Text format** to **Title case**, which will change the entered text so that each word of the name starts with a capital letter. Press **OK** to accept the changes.

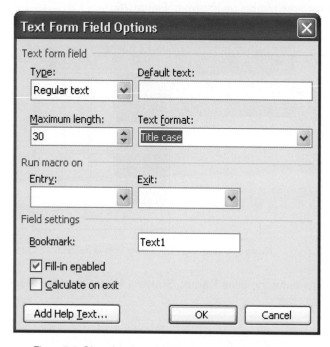

Figure 7.4: Changing the maximum length for a text form field

It may not be a good idea to restrict a name field to title case in general, since it will change **McIntosh** to **Mcintosh**, and so on.

For the meal selections, we are going to use drop-down lists so that people can select only those courses that are on the menu.

Drop-Down
Form Field

Place your insertion point in the next blank cell and press the **Drop-Down Form Field** button. As with the text field, a grey rectangle appears.

Double-click the field. The **Drop-Down Form Field Options** dialogue appears.

In the **Drop-down item** field, type **Garlic mushrooms**, then click the **Add** button (or press the **Enter** key). Repeat this for the other two options for the starter: **Leek and potato soup** and **Chicken liver pate**. The dialogue should look like Figure 7.5. Press **OK**.

Figure 7.5: Adding entries to a drop-down field on a form

TIP

You can use the up and down arrows on the right-hand side of the dialogue to change the position of the currently selected item in the list.

 Create two more drop-downs representing the options for the main course (**Roast turkey, Lamb shank, Dover sole** and **Butternut squash ravioli**) and dessert (**Christmas pudding, Ice cream, Chocolate mousse** and **Selection of cheeses**) respectively.

For the **Dates Available**, people should be able to select which of the 5th, 6th or 7th of December would be convenient for them. Because it is valid to be able to choose more than one, a drop-down list will not do; instead, three separate checkboxes are more appropriate.

 In the final empty table cell, type the text **5th December** followed by a few spaces. Then click the **Check Box Form Field** button.

 Press the **Enter** key, and create two more lines with checkboxes for the 6th and 7th December.

The form should look like Figure 7.6.

˙Christmas·Dinner·Orders¶

This·year's·Christmas·Dinner·will·be·at·the·Plough·and·Furrow·on·the·5th,·
6th·or·7th·of·December·(whichever·day·most·people·can·make).¶

¶

Please·fill·in·the·following·form·with·your·food·preferences,·and·return·it·
to·me·by·the·end·of·this·week.¶

Name:¤	○○○○○¤	¤
Starter:¤	Garlic mushrooms¤	¤
Main·Course:¤	Roast turkey¤	¤
Dessert:¤	Christmas pudding¤	¤
Dates·Available:¤	5th·December···▢¶	¤
	6th·December···▢¶	
	7th·December···▢¤	

¶

Figure 7.6: Form with three different field types

So far, the form isn't interactive: there are just a few static bits of grey text. To get the form into a state fit to send out, it needs to be **protected** against changes, which will activate the form fields.

Protect
Form

 Click the **Protect Form** button. This changes the whole nature of the form – you can no longer edit the document apart from the form's fields, which have now been activated.

> **Syllabus Ref: AM3.4.2.4**
> Protect a form.

 Try out the fields. Check that you can't enter more than 30 characters in the name field, and see what happens when you enter a name in all lower case letters. Try out the drop-down lists and the checkboxes.

 Save the document as **Christmas Dinner Orders.doc** and close it.

Let's edit the form to give another possible date.

 Reload the form document and add text and a checkbox for 8th December. Remember that you will need to unprotect the form (click the **Protect Form** button again) before you can edit it; don't forget to protect it again when you have finished.

> **TIP**
>
> To unprotect a form you will need the **Forms** toolbar. If it is not visible, use **View, Toolbars, Forms** to display it.

Note!

To delete a field from a form, simply select the field and press **Delete**. This is the same technique used to delete any fields from a Word document. Remember this, since you may be asked to delete a field in the exam.

TIP

As with any other type of editing, you must unprotect a form before you can delete any of its fields. If you use **File**, **Save As** you can save a form in a particular folder and choose a format to convert it into, such as **html** if you wish to use the form on a web page.

 Save the modified document and close the **Forms** toolbar.

Comments

Forms are one aspect of sharing information using Word, when you have specific information you want to capture. Another scenario in which several people will edit the same document is when that document is sent out for review. Word has two features that help the review process: the ability for people to add **comments** to parts of the document, and the ability to **track changes** so that it is easy to see at a glance what has changed.

Let's try out these features, **comments** first. Suppose you've written the first draft of the Master Brain letter, but want your colleague to check through it before you send it out.

 Open the file **Master Brain.doc**, which you created in Chapter 5.

Before you pass it on to your colleague, you want to make a couple of notes that explain the text, but won't appear on the printed version of the letter.

 From the menu, select **View**, **Toolbars** and tick the **Reviewing** option if it is not already ticked. The **Reviewing** toolbar will be displayed.

Figure 7.7: Reviewing toolbar

Insert Comment

 Click in the margin to the left of the text **[Click here and type recipient's address]** to select it. Press the **Insert Comment** button on the **Reviewing** toolbar.

> **Syllabus Ref: AM3.1.4.1**
> Add or remove text comments.

The text to which the new comment applies is highlighted, and joined by a dotted line to space for the new comment in the margin.

 Type the comment **This will be filled in by mail merge from the contestant database.**

 Select the first **£500** in the text and add another comment saying **Please check.**

The document should now look like Figure 7.8.

Master Brain¶

Master·Brain·10ᵗʰ·Anniversary·Show¶
Unit·7¶
Smartypants·Lane¶
Cleverton¶
BR4·1NY¶

2·November,·05¶

[Click·**here**·and·type·recipient's·address]¶ .... **Comment [MJS1]:** This·will·be·filled·in·by·mail·merge·from·the·contestant·database.¶

Dear·Sir·or·Madam:¶

Master·Brain·will·be·ten·years·old·this·spring!·To·celebrate,·we·are·planning·several·special·anniversary·shows·where·previous·contestants·can·again·pit·their·wits·against·the·Memory·Bank·for·a·cash·prize·of·up·to·£500.¶ .... **Comment [MJS2]:** Please·check.¶

If·you·would·like·to·take·part[],·or·to·discuss·the·details,·please·contact·me·at·the·address·given·at·the·top·of·this·letter,·giving·your·name·and·a·daytime·contact·telephone·number.·Remember,·you·could·win·£500?¶

We·look·forward·to·seeing·you·in·the·spring.··Good·luck!¶

▪ Sincerely,¶

▪

Annie·Versary¶
▪ Researcher¶

Figure 7.8: A document with comments

 TIP

To change the initials used for the comment numbers, go to **Tools**, **Options**, **User Information**, and set the **Initials** value.

Tracking changes

Before passing the document on to your colleague, you should turn on **track changes**. This will allow him or her to edit the document, but make it obvious to you what changes are made. You will then have the final decision of whether or not to accept each of those changes.

 From the menu select **Tools, Track Changes**. That's all there is to it!

If you're learning with other people then it would be a good idea to swap documents at this stage, to make the review process more realistic. However, if you are learning on your own you will still be able to work through the exercise.

You are now acting as the reviewer, looking at a document that has been sent to you for comments.

 Edit the address: double-click the word **Lane** to select it, and with it still selected type **Road**. Add the country **United Kingdom** to the bottom.

Because track changes is on, the address should look like Figure 7.9. Notice the vertical change bars to the left of each of the modified lines (including the post code, which has changed because you pressed **Enter** at the end of it to insert a new line). Word highlights new text by colouring and underlining it; the text you deleted is remembered and shown as a comment.

```
Master·Brain·10ᵗʰ·Anniversary·Show¶
Unit·7¶
Smartypants·Road¶
Cleverton¶ ▾
BR4·1NY¶
United·Kingdom¶
```
Deleted: Lane

Figure 7.9: Editing text with 'track changes' on

 Click in the margin to the left of **Dear Sir or Madam** to select it, and insert a comment saying **Can you get this from the database too?**

 Click in the comment **Please check** (which has now been renumbered to 3) and edit it to say **This is correct.**

 Edit the second paragraph of the letter, adding **, email address (if you have one)** after **giving your name.**

Master Brain¶

Master·Brain·10th·Anniversary·Show¶
Unit·7¶
Smartypants·Road¶
Cleverton¶
BR4·1NY¶
United·Kingdom¶

> **Deleted:** Lane

2·November,·05¶

[Click·**here**·and·type·recipient's·address]¶

Dear·Sir·or·Madam,¶

> **Comment [MJS1]:** This·will·be·filled·in·by·mail·merge·from·the·contestant·database.¶

Master· Brain· will· be· ten· years· old· this· spring!· To· celebrate,· we· are· planning· several· special· anniversary·shows·where·previous·contestants·can·again·pit·their·wits·against·the·Memory·Bank· for·a·cash·prize·of·up·to·£500.¶

> **Comment [REV2]:** Can·you·get·this·from·the·database·too?¶

> **Comment [MJS3]:** This·is·correct.¶

If·you·would·like·to·take·part¶,·or·to·discuss·the·details,·please·contact·me·at·the·address·given·at· the· top· of· this· letter,· giving· your· name,· email· address· (if· you· have· one)· and· a· daytime· contact· telephone·number.·Remember,·you·could·win·£500?¶¶

We·look·forward·to·seeing·you·in·the·spring.·Good·luck!¶

▪ Sincerely,¶

▪

Annie·Versary¶
▪ Researcher¶
¶

Figure 7.10: Letter with review comments

Accepting or rejecting changes

Having had your document reviewed, it is time to switch **track changes** off again, which means that you must decide which of the changes to keep and which to 'roll back'.

> **Syllabus Ref: AM3.1.4.4**
> Accept or reject changes in a document.

> Now is the time to swap back documents if you are learning with other people.

Track Changes

Click the **Track Changes** button on the **Reviewing** toolbar. You can now edit the document without the changes being marked. Unlike with earlier versions of Word, you can turn track changes off without having to make an instant decision about which changes to keep.

With your insertion point anywhere in the letter, press **Ctrl+Home**. This is a quick way of jumping to the beginning of a document.

Next

Press the **Next** button on the **Reviewing** toolbar. This will highlight the first change in the document, the deleted **Lane**.

Accept Change

Press the **Accept Change** button. The comment bubble containing the deleted text will disappear.

Click on the text **United Kingdom**. We are going to reject this change – having the country in the address is unnecessary, because all of the former contestants are already in the UK. Press the **Reject Change** button.

Reject Change

The text **United Kingdom** disappears from the document. You are happy with the rest of the proposed changes, so decide to accept all of them in one go.

 Click the **arrow** to the right of the **Accept Change** button. This reveals a drop-down menu. Select **Accept All Changes in Document**, as shown in Figure 7.11.

Figure 7.11: Accepting all remaining changes in the document

Syllabus Ref: AM3.1.4.1

Add or remove text comments.

Finally, let's look at the comments now in the document. The first two are useful to keep as reminders for when we do the mail merge in Chapter 10. The third is simply a response to a query about whether the prize value was correct, so we can safely delete it.

 Right-click comment 3 and select **Delete Comment** from the menu that appears.

The final document with the accepted changes should look like Figure 7.12.

Master Brain¶

Master Brain 10ᵗʰ Anniversary Show¶
Unit 7¶
Smartypants Road¶
Cleverton¶
BR4 1NY¶

2 November, 05¶

[Click **here** and type recipient's address]¶

Dear Sir or Madam:¶

Comment [MJS1]: This will be filled in by mail merge from the contestant database.¶

Comment [REV2]: Can you get this from the database too?¶

Master Brain will be ten years old this spring! To celebrate, we are planning several special anniversary shows where previous contestants can again pit their wits against the Memory Bank for a cash prize of up to £500.¶

If you would like to take part, or to discuss the details, please contact me at the address given at the top of this letter, giving your name, email address (if you have one) and a daytime contact telephone number. Remember, you could win £500?!¶

We look forward to seeing you in the spring. Good luck!¶

▪ Sincerely,¶

▪

Annie Versary¶
▪ Researcher¶

Figure 7.12: Letter after review comments have been applied

Password protection

Since this chapter is all about sharing documents, it's worth mentioning password protection. You can assign a password to a document, which can then be opened only if you enter the correct password.

Although there is no particularly sensitive information in the letter, let's use it to try out password protection.

> **Syllabus Ref: AM3.3.5.1**
> Add password protection to a document.

 From the menu select **Tools**, **Options** and change to the **Security** tab.

 In the **Password to open** field, type **password**. Rather than seeing the characters you type, you just get a bullet symbol for each, as shown in Figure 7.13. You wouldn't use such an obvious password if you really wanted to protect your document, but it will do to demonstrate the concept. Press **OK**.

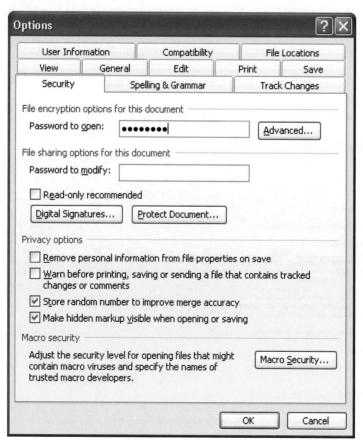

Figure 7.13: Protecting a document with a password

As a double-check that you have entered your password correctly, a **Confirm Password** dialogue appears, as shown in Figure 7.14. Type **password** again and press **OK**.

Figure 7.14: Confirming that you typed the password correctly

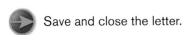 Save and close the letter.

 Reload the letter (it should be at the top of your **recently used files** list in Word's **File** menu). The **Password** dialogue shown in Figure 7.15 appears.

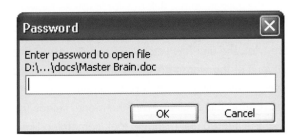

Figure 7.15: Opening a password-protected document

 To prove that the password protection works, just press **OK** without entering the password. You should get an error message like that in Figure 7.16.

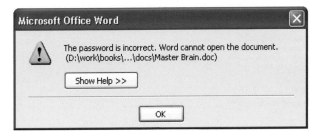

Figure 7.16: Oops, wrong password!

 Press **OK** on the error dialogue to close it, then reload the document. This time type **password**, and then press **OK**. The document should load as normal.

 To remove the password, select **Tools, Options** from the menu. The **Options** dialogue should open with the **Security** tab selected (because this was the last one you used) and the password highlighted. You can simply press **Delete** to delete the password and then press **OK**.

 Save and close the document, then reopen it. This time you should not need a password.

Test yourself

1. Create a form for ordering customised T-shirts. Include drop-down menus for the colour and size, a text entry field for the slogan, and a tick box for 'express delivery'.

2. Create a simple document containing the text to *Ten green bottles hanging on the wall* (tip: use **Cut** and **Paste** a lot; the first few verses will suffice). Save this document, then go through and change several of the words **green** to other colours instead. Also delete some words and add some new ones. Save the altered document with a different name. Close the changed document and reopen the original. From the menu, select **Tools, Compare and Merge Documents** and choose the altered file. It should look something like Figure 7.17. Practise accepting or rejecting each change.

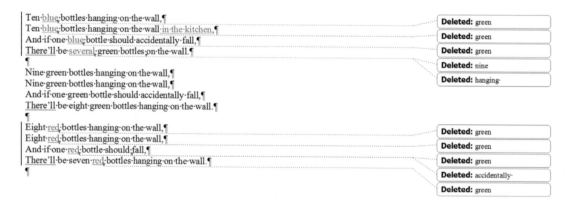

Figure 7.17: Merging documents to show the differences between them

8 Graphics

Introduction

This chapter introduces Word's **Drawing** toolbar. The exercise shows you step-by-step how to build up a diagram of a sailing boat, which forms the centre of a handout for your local sailing club.

In this chapter you will

- learn how to insert and move **clip art** to add a professional look to your documents

- create a drawing from the basic components in Word's **Drawing** toolbar

- see why it can be useful to **group** related drawing elements together, so that Word treats them as a unit

- apply **line** and **fill colours** to the drawing elements

- add **text boxes** to the diagram, and see how **text boxes** can be **linked** so that the text flows from one to another.

Inserting graphics

In this chapter you will create an A4 handout for your local sailing club. The handout will list the names of the main parts of a sailing boat.

We'll start by creating a new document and adding some basic text and graphics.

 Open a new document. Type the following two lines, setting the font to **Arial Rounded MT Bold** with size **24**.

Timbleton·Sailing·Club·Presents...¶
Lesson·1:·Parts·of·a·sailing·boat¶
¶

Figure 8.1: Introductory text for sailing information sheet

We want to insert a general picture relating to teaching or training, which will give a common look and feel to other information sheets produced by the club.

 From the menu, select **Insert**, **Picture**, **Clip Art**. The **Clip Art** task pane will appear.

 Under **Search for** type **teacher** then press **Go** (or the **Enter** key).

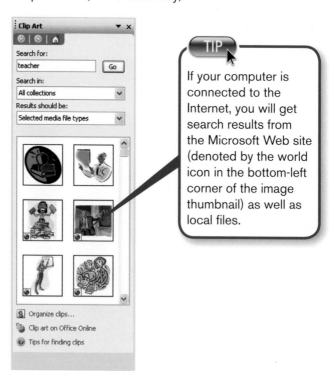

If your computer is connected to the Internet, you will get search results from the Microsoft Web site (denoted by the world icon in the bottom-left corner of the image thumbnail) as well as local files.

Figure 8.2: Selecting clip art to insert into the information sheet

Choose an image to insert into the document – I'm going to use the picture of the teacher at the board, but it doesn't really matter. Hover your mouse pointer over the image, which will display an arrow on the right-hand side. Click the arrow to reveal a menu, and select **Insert**.

Figure 8.3: Inserting clip art

The image appears in the document, but it would look a lot neater up in the top-right corner looking down on the heading text.

Syllabus Ref: AM3.4.5.5
Send pre-defined shapes in front of or behind text.

 Double-click the new picture to display the **Format Picture** dialogue. Select the **Layout** tab and set the **Wrapping style** to **Behind text**. Press **OK**.

Figure 8.4: Formatting picture layout

 TIP

If you want a picture to overlap text, but to be on top of it instead of behind, use the **In front of text** option.

Exactly the same technique is used for pre-defined shapes, which you will see in the next section.

Syllabus Ref: AM3.1.1.6
Use text wrapping options.

Sometimes you want text to flow around embedded objects, such as pictures, rather than just having it free floating in front of (or behind) them. Although we won't be using these options in this exercise, you can use the **Format Picture** dialogue's **Advanced** button to specify exactly how the text should behave.

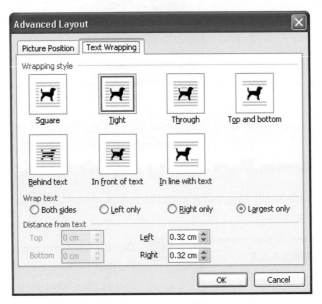

Figure 8.5: Options for wrapping text around graphics

The **Advanced Layout** dialogue has various options for text wrapping, as shown in Figure 8.5.

The **Wrapping style** icons show how each option behaves. The **Square** option prevents text from flowing into any part of the image's rectangle; the **Tight** option allows text to flow over any blank space on the left or right of the image; and the **Through** option will flow text through any blank space in the image. The **Top and bottom** wrapping style causes the flow of text to stop above the image and resume below it. The two options **Behind text** and **In front of text** you already know about. The option **In line with text** is the normal default text wrap, where the image is aligned with the baseline of the text that follows it.

The **Wrap text** options control which side of the picture is permitted to have text. The options **Both sides**, **Left only** and **Right only** act as you would expect; **Largest only** restricts the text to whichever side (left or right) has the most space.

The **Distance from text** options give you fine control over the border between the image and the text that flows around it.

Click the image and drag it into the top-right corner of the page. Click the bottom-left resize handle (a white circle) and drag it up and to the right to shrink the image, as shown in Figure 8.6.

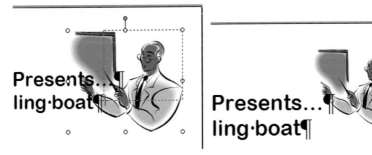

Figure 8.6: Resizing an image

As well as the white resize handles, you'll notice a green spot. You can drag this to rotate an image.

Let's try changing the image's border and background colour.

 Double-click the picture to open the **Format Picture** dialogue. Switch to the **Colors and Lines** tab. Select light blue as the **Fill Color** and make the **Line Color** red, dashed and **3 pt** in weight, as shown in Figure 8.7. Press **OK**.

Syllabus Ref: AM3.4.5.1
Modify image borders.

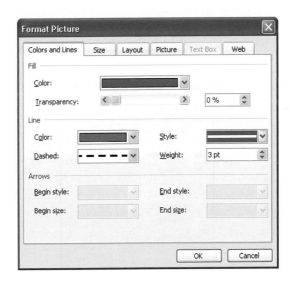

Figure 8.7: Changing border and shading options for a picture

In this case, the result is truly awful! You need to know how to change image borders for the exam, but for the sailing club's instruction sheet the original image was fine as it was.

 From the menu, select **Edit, Undo Format Drawing Object** (or type **Ctrl+Z**) to return the image to its original state.

Drawing in Word

As well as being able to insert pre-prepared images into a document, you can also create simple drawings from lines, circles, rectangles, and more complicated shapes, from within Word.

The following steps show you how to build up a picture of a sailing boat from some of the drawing tools that Word provides.

> **Syllabus Ref: AM3.4.5.2**
>
> Create a simple drawing using the drawing options.

 From the menu, select **View**, **Toolbars**, and tick **Drawing** if it isn't already ticked. The **Drawing** toolbar appears.

Figure 8.8: The Drawing toolbar

The first thing to do is check that the drawing tools are set up to **snap to grid** (the equivalent of drawing on graph paper by connecting up the points where the lines cross), rather than drawing completely freehand. With **snap to grid** it is much easier to get elements to line up properly.

 From the **Drawing** toolbar, select **Draw**, **Grid**. Check that **Snap objects to grid** is ticked and press **OK**.

Figure 8.9: Checking the grid settings

We'll start by drawing the sails. At this stage, the relative sizes of the various components are more important than their actual sizes: we can resize the whole image when it's finished.

The following exercise expects a drawing canvas to be automatically created whenever you add a drawing object. This is determined by an option, so let's make sure that it's turned on.

 TIP

Some people find this feature annoying. You might like to turn the setting off again after you finish working through this chapter.

 From the menu, select **Tools, Options**. In the **General** tab, make sure that the option **Automatically create drawing canvas when inserting AutoShapes** is ticked.

Syllabus Ref: AM3.4.5.3
Use pre-defined shapes options.

 Position your insertion point after the text that is already on the page. From the **Drawing** toolbar, select **AutoShapes, Basic Shapes** and then click on the **Right Triangle** icon, as shown in Figure 8.10.

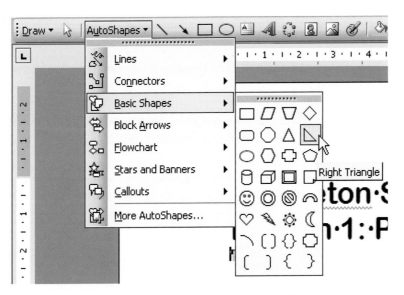

Figure 8.10: Inserting a right-angled triangle

A drawing canvas appears in the document, with the text **Create your drawing here**. Note that you are not constrained to drawing in this area – you could draw the triangle anywhere you liked on the page and the empty canvas would disappear – but a drawing canvas makes it easier to arrange and resize objects in the drawing.

Press and hold your left mouse button in the middle of the drawing canvas. Drag your mouse down and to the right before releasing the button to produce a 'mainsail', as shown in Figure 8.11.

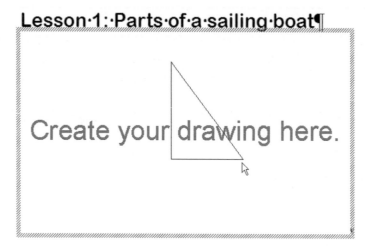

Figure 8.11: Starting to draw a sailing boat

We also need a smaller 'jib' sail, facing in the opposite direction.

 Use the **AutoShapes** menu again to draw another triangle. At this stage the size and location aren't important, as you will be resizing and moving it shortly.

 With the new triangle still selected, click **Draw** on the **Drawing** toolbar and select **Rotate or Flip, Flip Horizontal**.

 You can drag the triangle to move it (it has to be the triangle itself, not the blank area that is also bounded by the white resize handles) and resize it by dragging the resize handles so that your picture resembles Figure 8.12.

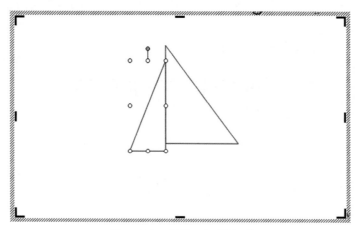

Figure 8.12: Adding the 'jib' sail

The next step is to add the body of the craft.

 Add another **AutoShape**: the **Trapezoid**, the third button on the top row of the **Basic Shapes** selection. Make it long and thin, like the body of a sailing boat.

Trapezoid

The three shapes you now have give a rough impression of a boat shape. One of the items that you will need to highlight on the finished diagram is the foredeck; this will be much easier to see in three dimensions. Word has a **3-D Style** tool that will make it easy to add depth to the picture.

 With the **trapezoid** selected, click the **3-D Style** tool on the **Drawing** toolbar and select **3-D Style 2**, as shown in Figure 8.13.

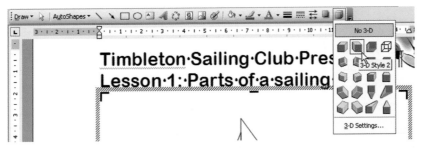

Figure 8.13: Applying a 3-D style to an AutoShape

 Still with the trapezoid selected, move the yellow handle; this adjusts the angle of the slope. Reduce this angle so that you can see some of the front of the boat, as in Figure 8.14.

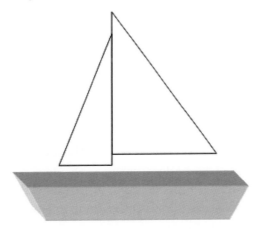

Figure 8.14: Sailing boat with a 3-D body

 To add to the 3-D effect, extend the mast so that it touches the body: click the **Line** tool, then click and drag from the right-angle corner of the lower sail vertically down to the centre of the deck.

Line

You also need to represent the cabin space.

Parallel-ogram

 Add a new **AutoShape**, this time a **Parallelogram** (the second **Basic Shape**).

Flip the new shape horizontally and position it as shown in Figure 8.15. It is important that you make sure it overlaps slightly with the mast (see the next step). Word will prevent you from making the shape very thin, so get it in roughly the right position, as thin as you can, then **double-click** the shape and use the **Size** tab to reduce the **Height** to **60%**. You should also use the yellow handle to adjust the angle of the parallelogram to match the 3-D effect of the body.

TIP

Hold down the **Alt** key to temporarily override the **snap to grid**.

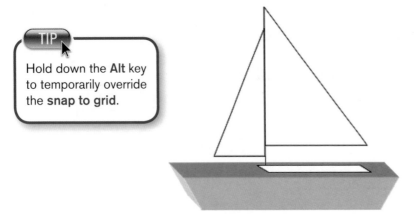

Figure 8.15: Boat with mast and cabin

Order of drawing elements

Each of the elements in a drawing has an **order** associated with it, so that Word knows which objects to draw first. Solid shapes will obscure other shapes with a lower order. Each new element you draw has a higher order than those that have gone before, but you can change the order of any of the elements to get the effect you need.

 If you have positioned the cabin correctly, it will have obscured part of the mast you drew (see Figure 8.16). Select the mast line and from the **Drawing** toolbar select **Draw**, **Order**, **Bring to Front** as shown in Figure 8.17.

> **Syllabus Ref: AM3.4.5.4**
> Send pre-defined shape to back or front.

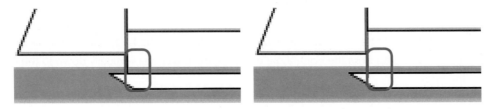

Figure 8.16: The mast line (a) behind the cabin and (b) brought to the front

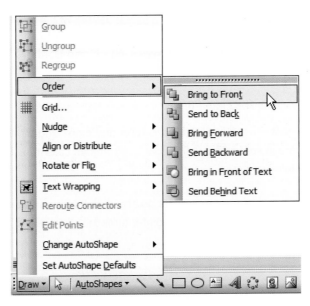

Figure 8.17: Bringing a shape to the front

 Create another trapezoid and place it as shown in Figure 8.18. This represents the centreboard, which keeps the boat stable in the water.

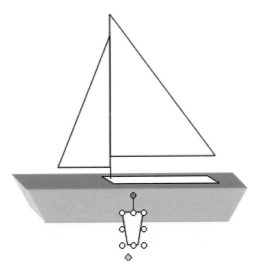

Figure 8.18: Adding the centreboard

 To create the rudder, hold down the **Ctrl** key while you drag the centreboard trapezoid to the back of the boat – this will create a copy.

Select both of the trapezoids (select one, hold down **Ctrl**, then select the other) and from the **Drawing** toolbar select **Draw, Order, Send to Back**.

The final element to add is the **burgee**, which is a flag at the top of the mast.

Wave

 From the **Drawing** toolbar, select **AutoShapes**, **Stars and Banners**, **Wave**. Use this tool to draw a small flag at the top of the mast.

Your drawing should now look like Figure 8.19.

These sails are rather squat – a real sailing boat is taller and more elegant. Let's make the sails taller. First, let's make sure there is space above the boat to stretch its sails into. If your drawing is near the top of its frame, do the following step.

 Select the drawing and hover your mouse pointer over the thick black line in the top-middle of the graphics frame, so that your mouse pointer turns into an inverted **T** shape. Click and drag upwards to expand the frame.

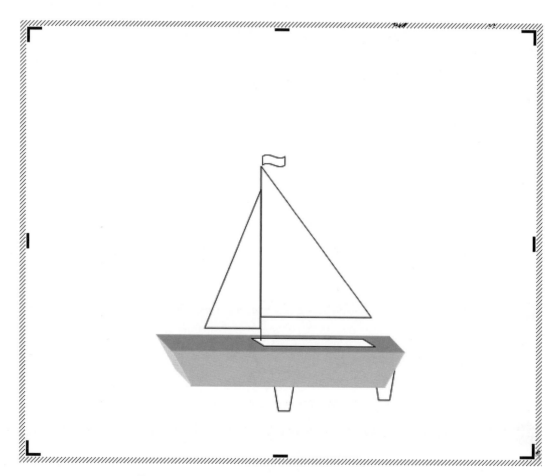

Figure 8.19: Sailing boat with space above for stretching the sails

Grouping

 Click in a blank area of the frame to deselect everything, then select both sails and the burgee by dragging a rectangle across them (or you could use the **Shift** key and click on each in turn).

 Click on the top-centre selection handle of any of the three selected elements and drag it upwards.

This resizes all of the selected elements in one go, without repositioning them, as shown in Figure 8.20. This is not exactly the behaviour we want, since the burgee has been stranded half-mast!

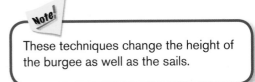
Note! These techniques change the height of the burgee as well as the sails.

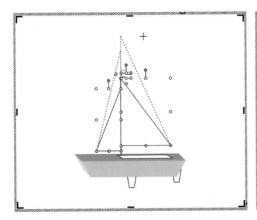 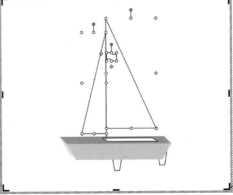

Figure 8.20: Resizing a selection of drawing elements does not move them relative to one another

To get the burgee to move relative to the resized sails, we have to tell Word to treat the three drawing elements as a **group**.

 From the menu, select **Edit, Undo Resize Object**, to return the drawing to its 'squat' state.

> **Syllabus Ref: AM3.4.5.6**
> Group or ungroup pre-defined shapes.

 With the three drawing elements still selected, from the **Drawing** toolbar select **Draw, Group**.

The three sets of selection handles are replaced by a single set, bounding all three elements. The sails and the burgee will now be treated as a **group** by Word.

Click on the top-centre **selection handle** for the **group** and drag it upwards. This time, the burgee moves **relative** to the other elements in the **group**, as shown in Figure 8.21.

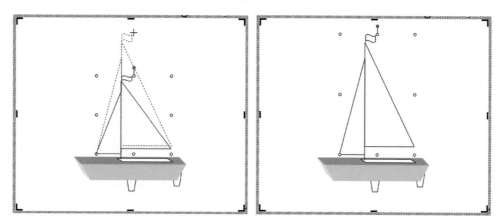

Figure 8.21: Resizing grouped elements – the individual elements move relative to one another

You can create a hierarchy of groups, so that related items are grouped together and those components are in turn grouped. Let's **ungroup** the three elements and create the more fundamental grouping of the two sails as a base component.

 With the group selected, from the **Drawing** toolbar select **Draw, Ungroup**. The three components now have their individual selection handles returned.

 Click in a blank space to clear the selection, and select just the two sails. **Group** them together.

 With the group you have just created, additionally select the burgee and the bottom of the mast. **Group** these three elements together.

 Clear the selection and then drag across the remaining elements that constitute the body of the sailing boat, and **Group** these.

 Finally, **Group** together the two components (the 'sails' component and the 'body' component).

Let's add some colour.

Even though the elements have been grouped, you can still select individual elements to work with: click on the burgee and it will be displayed with grey **selection handles**.

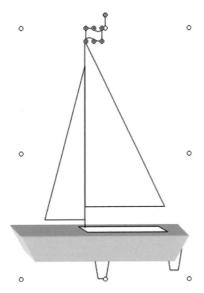

Figure 8.22: Selecting a component within a group

 Double-click the burgee to display the **Format AutoShape** dialogue (also available from the right-click menu). In the **Colors and Lines** tab set the **Fill Color** to **Red** and press **OK**.

Apply colours to each of the other components so that your sailing boat looks like Figure 8.23.

Figure 8.23: Coloured drawing

Text boxes

The final task is to add the text labels to the diagram, to give names to the different parts of the sailing boat. The easiest way to do this is to use **text boxes**, which are rectangular drawing elements containing text.

Syllabus Ref: AM3.4.3.1
Insert or delete text boxes.

Text Box

 In the **Drawing** toolbar, click the **Text Box** icon. Click and drag a small rectangle somewhere in the drawing frame. The exact size doesn't matter, since you can change it later.

We want all of the labels to have the same colour scheme. The easiest thing to do is to change this first text box to have the **border** and **fill** colours we want; we can then **copy** it to create the others.

Syllabus Ref: AM3.4.3.3
Apply border and shading options in text boxes.

 With the text box selected, **double-click** its border. The **Format Text Box** dialogue will appear.

 Set the **Fill Color** to **No Fill** and select **No Line** as the **Line Color**, as shown in Figure 8.24. You could, of course, choose specific colours for one or both of these, but it is often useful to have an unboxed transparent label, so you need to know how to do this. Press **OK** to set the new colours.

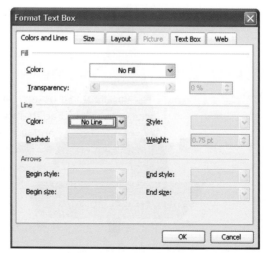

Figure 8.24: Changing border and fill options for a text box

 With your insertion point in the text box, use the drop-downs on the **Formatting** toolbar to change the font to 14pt Arial in blue, just as you would for the normal body text of a document.

In the text box, type the first label: **burgee**.

Figure 8.25: Adding a text box to the drawing

 To copy the text box, hold down the **Ctrl** key and drag the text box's border (**not** one of the handles). Your mouse pointer will have a **+** sign next to it, to show that you are **copying** instead of **moving** (see Figure 8.26) and when you release the mouse button you will have two text labels saying **burgee**.

Figure 8.26: Copying a text box by dragging it with the Ctrl key held down

Syllabus Ref: AM3.4.3.1
Edit, move, or resize text boxes.

 Click anywhere in the text of the copied text box and change it from **burgee** to **mainsail**. You do this in the same way as with any other text in your document.

TIP

You can treat text boxes just like any other drawing elements – you drag them about to move them, hold down the **Ctrl** key and drag to copy them, or resize them using their selection handles. When a text box is selected and you are not editing the text (that is, you have clicked on the border instead of in the text), you can press the **Delete** key to delete it.

 Use the **Line** tool from the **Drawing** toolbar to draw lines connecting the text labels to the appropriate parts of the drawing.

Line

 Copy and edit more labels, and link them to the picture with lines, so that your final diagram looks like Figure 8.27.

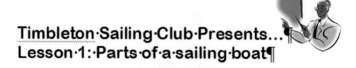

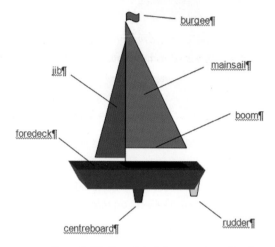

Figure 8.27: Completed diagram of a sailing boat

TIP

Remember that you can hold down the **Alt** key to override the **snap to grid** feature. This lets you position the lines accurately.

TIP

If you need to draw lots of the same type of drawing object, you can double-click the button in the **Drawing** toolbar. This button will stay selected until you click it again.

Linking text boxes

The final thing you need to know about text boxes is how to link them together, so that any text that won't fit in the first box is automatically flowed into the next, and so on down the chain.

 Create two small text boxes in the sailing boat diagram, one above the **jib** label and one below it.

 Select the first of these new text boxes. If the **Text Box** toolbar (see Figure 8.28) is not on display, select **View, Toolbars, Text Box** from the menu.

Figure 8.28: The Text Box toolbar

Syllabus Ref: AM3.1.1.7

Use text orientation options.

The rightmost button on the **Text Box** toolbar lets you change the **orientation** of the text. See also Chapter 6, page 103.

Syllabus Ref: AM3.4.3.4

Link text boxes.

 Click on the chain icon (**Create Text Box Link**) in the **Text Box** toolbar and then click on the second of the text boxes. This tells Word to flow into the second text box any text that won't fit in the first.

 Type some text in the first text box, as shown in Figure 8.29. When the text gets too big for the first box, it should overflow to the second.

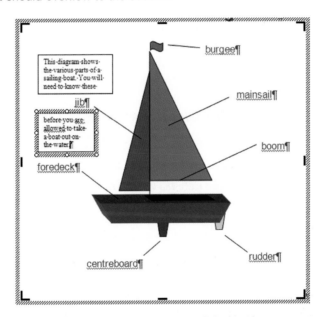

Figure 8.29: Flowing text between linked text boxes

WordArt

We used the **Style Gallery** in Chapter 3 to import styles from a template. Another text design gallery in Word is the **WordArt** dialogue. WordArt, as the name implies, is text that behaves like a graphic – meaning you can rotate it, flip it, and so on. Let's change the title of the handout to WordArt.

Syllabus Ref: AM3.1.1.8

Use available text design gallery options.

 Delete the text **Presents...** from the first line.

 Select the remainder of the first line, but not the paragraph mark after it.

 TIP

We are going to replace the selected text with a WordArt object. If you select the paragraph mark as well as the text then you will lose the clip art from the top-right corner.

Insert
WordArt

 Press the **Insert WordArt** button on the **Drawing** toolbar. The **WordArt Gallery** will appear.

 Select the third option (the arced text), as shown in Figure 8.30, and press **OK**.

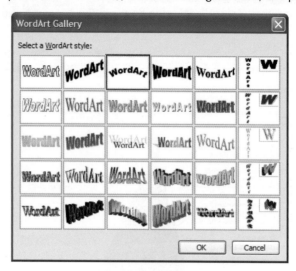

Figure 8.30: The WordArt Gallery

 The **Edit WordArt Text** dialogue appears, containing the text we had selected. Reduce the text size to **28**, as shown in Figure 8.31, and then press **OK**.

Figure 8.31: Setting the WordArt text and font options

Centre the new WordArt and the text line that follows it using the **Center** button on the **Formatting** toolbar.

Center

The handout should now look like Figure 8.32.

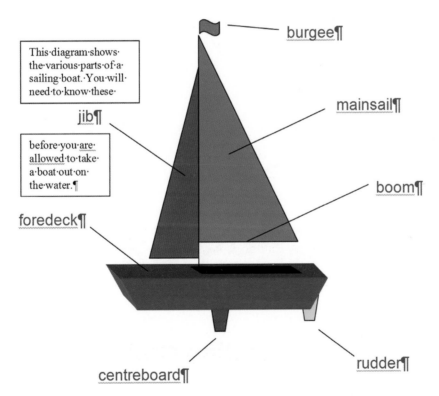

This diagram shows the various parts of a sailing boat. You will need to know these

jib¶

before you are allowed to take a boat out on the water.¶

foredeck¶

burgee¶

mainsail¶

boom¶

centreboard¶

rudder¶

Figure 8.32: Handout with WordArt heading

 Save your document as **Timbleton Sailing Club.doc**.

Test yourself

1. The **tiller** is missing from the diagram. The tiller is the stick connected to the rudder, and can be represented by a horizontal line from the centre back of the cabin to the very back of the boat. Draw a tiller in **red** and add a label for it to the diagram.

2. In a new document, try to create the casino logo shown in Figure 8.33. This isn't easy, so take your time. Start by creating the two playing cards as normal rectangles side-by-side: you can **group** the elements in each card later and rotate them. To get the symbols for suits, the easiest thing is to do **Insert**, **Symbol** at some point in the document's text – you will find the suit symbols towards the bottom of the **(normal text)** font – then **cut** the symbol. You should then insert **WordArt** and **paste** the symbol into the dialogue box. (By using **WordArt** instead of a text box, you can rotate the A♥ through 90 degrees twice to get the upside-down symbol). Use **WordArt** again for the casino's name.

Figure 8.33: A casino logo created using WordArt

9 Embedded Graphics

Introduction

This chapter shows you how to add two charts to the **Music Sales** document you created in Chapter 6. These charts will use two different types of embedded object: **Microsoft Graph Charts** and **Microsoft Excel Worksheets**.

In this chapter you will

- see how to quickly create a chart, as an embedded **Microsoft Graph** object, from data that is already in a table in your document

- update the chart to customise the way it looks and position it where you want it in relation to the document text

- embed a **Microsoft Excel Worksheet** into the document and use it to create a chart from some calculations

- apply **captions** to the two embedded objects.

About embedding

One of the strengths of **Windows** as an operating system is that it makes it easy to share information between applications: you can copy text that was sent to you in an email and paste it into a Word document; you can do a calculation in a spreadsheet and copy and paste the result into a PowerPoint presentation.

However, the integration of **Windows** applications goes beyond straightforward cut and paste. All of the **Microsoft Office** applications, and many more besides, support a technology called **Object Linking and Embedding** (**OLE**). All this means is that any of the applications can play host to objects created in any of the others; the host can display and print the embedded object, but if you edit it the original application takes over. You'll see how this works later.

The most common use for **OLE** is probably to insert a worksheet or chart from **Excel** (the spreadsheet component of **Microsoft Office**) into a **Word** document. There is also a more basic charting package – **Microsoft Graph** – which we will look at first.

> This system for embedding documents is very flexible: you could, for example, embed an Excel worksheet inside a Word document inside an Excel worksheet inside... I don't recommend you try this!

Let's add a bar chart to the Music Sales document, to show the units sold by various artists (a visual representation of the top table).

 Open **Music Sales.doc**.

 Select the **Artist** and **Certified Units** data from the top table (including the headings, but not the total), as shown in Figure 9.1. This will form the basis of the chart. From the menu, select **Edit, Copy**. Note that you could use the same technique to create a chart based on worksheet data that had been pasted into a document.

Rank	Artist	Certified·Units·(m)
1	The·Beatles	166.5
2	Elvis·Presley	117.5
3	Led·Zeppelin	106.0
4	Garth·Brooks	105.0
5	The·Eagles	88.0
6	Billy·Joel	78.5
7	Pink·Floyd	73.5
8	Barbra·Streisand	71.5
9	Elton·John	67.5
10	Aerosmith	64.0
		938.0

Figure 9.1: Selecting data from which to create a chart

Although we want the chart in the top right, it will be easier to create it at the end of the document and then move it up later (you'll see why).

Syllabus Ref: AM3.4.4.2

Create a chart from a table or pasted worksheet data in a document.

Place your text insertion point on a blank line at the end of the document and from the menu select **Insert, Picture, Chart**.

A **chart** appears, together with a **Datasheet** window. This contains some dummy data, which you can replace; the **chart** will update itself whenever the **Datasheet** changes.

Top·10·Albums¶

Table·2:·Biggest-selling·albums·of·all·time·in·the·USA¶

Rank	Artist	Full·Title		Label	Sales· (m)
		Title	Subtitle		
1	The·Eagles	Eagles	Their·Greatest·Hits· 1971-1975	Elektra	28
2	Michael· Jackson	Thriller		Epic	26
3	Pink·Floyd	The·Wall		Columbia	23
4	Led·Zeppelin	Led·Zeppelin· IV		Swan·Song	22
5	Billy·Joel	Greatest·Hits	Volume·I·&·Volume·II	Columbia	21
6	Fleetwood· Mac	Rumours		Warner·Bros.	19
7	AC/DC	Back·in·B			
8	The·Beatles	The·Beat			
9	Shania·Twain	Come·on· Over			
10	Boston	Boston			

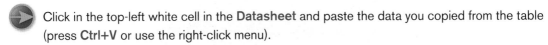

D:\work\books\ECDL Advance... - Datasheet

		A	B	C	D	E
		1st Qtr	2nd Qtr	3rd Qtr	4th Qtr	
1	East	20.4	27.4	90	20.4	
2	West	30.6	38.6	34.6	31.6	
3	North	45.9	46.9	45	43.9	

Figure 9.2: Inserting a chart object into a document

Click in the top-left white cell in the **Datasheet** and paste the data you copied from the table (press **Ctrl+V** or use the right-click menu).

You no longer need the dummy information from columns **B, C** and **D**, so select them by dragging across their header cells, then press **Delete**. Make sure you delete the three unneeded columns, not just blank out the data they hold, or Word will think that there are still four groups of columns and all of your data will be squashed up on the left-hand side of your graph.

To tidy up the datasheet so that the contents fit in the cells, double-click the border between the header cell **A** and the blank grey cell to its left. Do the same between the header cells **A** and **B**.

Your datasheet and its associated graph should now look similar to Figure 9.3.

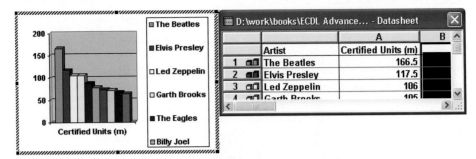

Figure 9.3: Data pasted into Datasheet

Notice that the chart has ten columns, but the legend on its right cannot fit all of the items in at present. Ultimately we want to move this chart to the top of the page, to the right of the 'Top 10 Artists' table. Before we can do this, let's make it the right size to fit in the available gap, and make sure that all of the artist names are listed in the legend.

 Resize the chart by dragging its bottom-right selection handle to make it roughly the right size for the gap we want to move it into. Click on the legend itself and increase its size if possible.

 Double-click the legend to display the **Format Legend** dialogue. In the **Font** tab, make sure the **Font Size** is **8** and that **Auto scale** is **not** ticked. Press **OK**.

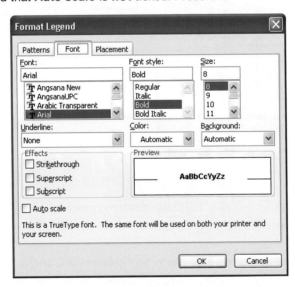

Figure 9.4: Changing the font size so that everything fits in the legend

 TIP

If you tick **AutoScale** then the font size used by the legend will change whenever you resize the chart. Unfortunately, this automatic scaling isn't very good, as you've already seen (remember that we're changing the font size manually because the automatic scaling didn't fit).

You should get a chart that looks like Figure 9.5.

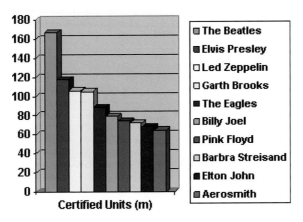

Figure 9.5: Chart with full legend

Since there's only one category of items in the chart, it will look better if we move the title **Certified Units (m)** so that it runs along the **Y-axis** instead of the **X-axis**.

 Click on the outside of the chart to select the **Chart Area** (the selection handles will bound everything, as shown in Figure 9.6). **Right-click** and select **Chart Options** from the menu.

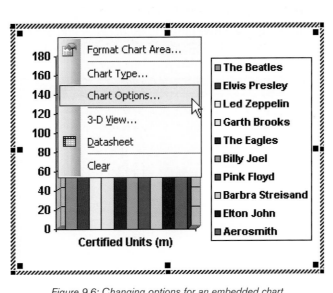

Figure 9.6: Changing options for an embedded chart

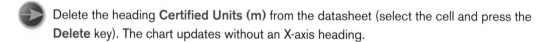

For the **Value (Z) axis** type **Certified Units (m)**, as shown in Figure 9.7, and press **OK**.

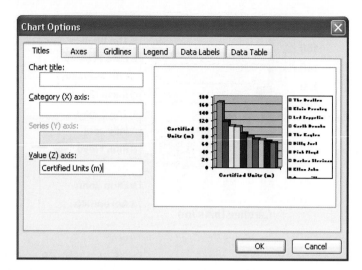

Figure 9.7: Changing the value axis

Delete the heading **Certified Units (m)** from the datasheet (select the cell and press the **Delete** key). The chart updates without an X-axis heading.

Double-click the **Value Axis Title** to display the **Format Axis Title** dialogue. Switch to the **Alignment** tab and change the **Orientation** to **90** degrees (the easiest way is to drag the red symbol to the top of the **Orientation** area) as shown in Figure 9.8. Press **OK**.

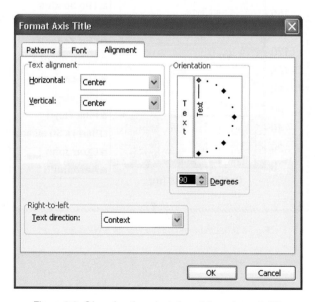

Figure 9.8: Changing the orientation of the value axis title

The chart should now look like Figure 9.9.

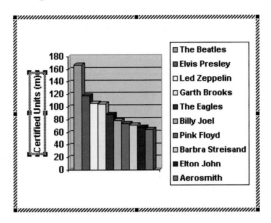

Figure 9.9: Chart with vertically orientated value axis title

 Click in any blank space in the document. This switches you out of edit mode: the **chart frame** and **Datasheet** disappear and the chart now acts very much like an embedded picture.

We now intend to position the chart to the right of the table to which it refers, so we must set it to float in front of the document's text and then drag it to its new position.

Syllabus Ref: AM3.4.4.4
Position a chart in a document.

 Right-click the chart and choose **Format Object** from the menu. The **Format Object** dialogue appears.

 Switch to the **Layout** tab and select **In front of text** as the **Wrapping style**, as shown in Figure 9.10. Press **OK**.

Figure 9.10: Floating an embedded object in front of document text

TIP

If you wanted to position an embedded object within normal document text, rather than next to a table, then you could use one of the other options to get the text to wrap around the object.

 Click and drag the chart to the right of the first of the two tables.

Top·10·Artists¶

- Table·1·:·Biggest-selling·artists·of·all·time·in·the·USA,·based·on·album·sales¶

Rank	Artist	Certified·Units·(m)
1	The·Beatles	166.5
2	Elvis·Presley	117.5
3	Led·Zeppelin	106.0
4	Garth·Brooks	105.0
5	The·Eagles	88.0
6	Billy·Joel	78.5
7	Pink·Floyd	73.5
8	Barbra·Streisand	71.5
9	Elton·John	67.5
10	Aerosmith	64.0
		938.0

Figure 9.11: Chart positioned next to the table to which it refers

Syllabus Ref: AM3.4.4.1
Modify an embedded worksheet in a document.

You can edit an embedded object by double-clicking it. The application associated with that type of file then takes over Word's toolbars and menus, and you can change the object.
When you have finished, click anywhere in the document outside the edited object to accept the changes and return control to Word.

Let's try this out by temporarily changing the values in the chart's **Datasheet**.

 Double-click the chart object. Change the sales value associated with **The Beatles** to **200** and notice how the graph is updated to reflect this.

 Click in a blank area of the document. The chart object is updated with its new value.

 Use the same method to change the sales value for **The Beatles** back to **166.5**.

Embedding Excel objects

If you have **Microsoft Excel** installed on your PC, you will often find it convenient to embed Excel charts and worksheets into Word documents. Excel is much more powerful than **Microsoft Graph** (used so far in this chapter), so you can perform complex calculations, and, of course, if you already have Excel objects that you want to use in documents then it makes sense to use them directly.

We are going to use Excel to draw a **pie chart** that shows the breakdown by label of album sales in the second table (notice that Elektra and Epic both have two entries in the top ten).

Although you will, in effect, be using Excel within Word, don't worry too much about the Excel functions themselves. Remember that you are studying for an exam in Word, not Excel, so in the exam you shouldn't be asked to do anything that requires in-depth knowledge of Excel.

 Select the whole of the **Label** and **Sales (m)** columns, including the headers, from the second table, and from the menu select **Edit, Copy**.

 Place your insertion point at the end of the document, making sure that there is at least one blank line between the table and your insertion point.

 From the menu, select **Insert, Object**. The **Object** dialogue appears. With the **Create New** tab displayed, choose **Microsoft Excel Worksheet**, as shown in Figure 9.12, and then press **OK**.

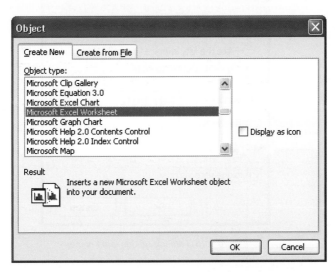

Figure 9.12: Inserting an Excel worksheet into a document

You can use the method given here to embed any type of object. For an Excel worksheet, you will find it quicker to use the **Insert Microsoft Excel Worksheet** button on the **Standard** toolbar.

An Excel worksheet appears in the document. It seems to overlap the bottom of the table above it, but that is because of the row and column headers, which are displayed only when editing.

 With worksheet cell **A1** selected (the default) select **Edit**, **Paste** from the menu.

The two rows you copied from the table appear in columns **A** and **B** of the worksheet. Before creating the pie chart, we need to consolidate this information so that there is only one entry for each of the record labels. We will do this using a filter – you don't need to remember how to do this for the exam.

 Click on one of the unselected cells (such as **D1**) to clear the selection, and then click and drag over cells **A1** to **A12** to select them.

 From the menu, select **Data**, **Filter**, **Advanced Filter** to display the **Advanced Filter** dialogue. If you get a warning dialogue, just **OK** it.

 Set the **Action** to **Copy to another location**. Make sure that **List range** is set to **$A$1:$A$12** and type **D1** for the **Copy to** location. Tick **Unique records only** (which is the whole point) and press **OK**.

Figure 9.13: Filtering unique label names

This was an automated way of getting a list of the labels with the duplicates removed. You could have typed the list by hand, but it makes sense to get Excel to do the work for you. Your worksheet should now look like Figure 9.14.

	A	B	C	D	E	F	G
1	*Label*	*Sales (m)*		*Label*			
2							
3	Elektra	28		Elektra			
4	Epic	26		Epic			
5	Columbia	23		Columbia			
	Swan	22		Swan			
6	Song			Song			
	Columbia	21		Warner			
7				Bros.			
	Warner	19		Capitol			
8	Bros.						
	Elektra	19		Mercury			
9				Nashville			
10	Capitol	19					

Sheet1

Figure 9.14: Worksheet showing a copied list of labels without duplicates

Now we need to add another column to hold the total sales for each label, which we'll calculate from columns **A** and **B**.

 Copy cell **B1** and paste it into cell **E1**. This creates a header for our new column.

The following two steps are just to tidy things up a bit.

 Click in cell **B3** and do a **copy**. Select cells **E3** to **E9**, then **right-click** and from the menu select **Paste Special**. The **Paste Special** dialogue appears.

 Set **Paste** to **Formats** and press **OK**. This sets the new cells to have blue text on a grey background, like the others.

Figure 9.15: Copying formatting information between cells

Click in cell **E3** and type **=SUMIF($A$3:$A$12, D3, $B$3:$B$12)** and press **Enter**. This tells Excel to sum all of the sales figures from column **B** that have a label (column **A**) that matches the value of cell **D3** (**Elektra**). You should get the result **47** (28 + 19).

 Click on cell **E3** again. Hover over the bottom-right corner of the selected cell so that your mouse pointer becomes a black cross, then click and drag down the rest of the column to cell **E9**, as shown in Figure 9.16.

Figure 9.16: Copying a formula across a range of cells (copy in progress)

This should copy the formula down, automatically generating the other totals: **43**, **44**, **22**, **19**, **19**, and **19**. These are not quite in numerical order, but this is easy to achieve:

 Select cells **D3** to **E9** by dragging over them. From the menu select **Data**, **Sort** to display the **Sort** dialogue. Set **Sort by** to **Column E** and choose **Descending**. Make sure that **My data range has** is set to **No header row** and press **OK**.

Figure 9.17: Sorting data in the embedded worksheet

The **Columbia** and **Epic** entries change order, so that the list is now in sales order, largest to smallest. Now we can use this data as the basis for a **pie chart**.

 With cells **D3** to **E9** still selected, choose **Insert, Chart** from the menu. The **Chart Wizard** appears.

 Select **Pie** as the **Chart type** and select the second **Chart sub-type – Pie with a 3-D visual effect** – as shown in Figure 9.18. Press **Next**.

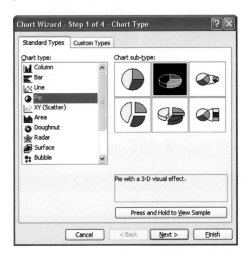

Figure 9.18: Selecting a chart type

 Because of the cells you had selected before starting the **Chart Wizard**, it should automatically detect that the data range is **=Sheet1!$D$3:$E$9** and that the series are in **Columns**, as shown in Figure 9.19. Press **Next**.

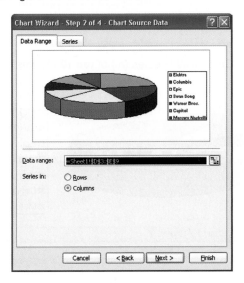

Figure 9.19: The default settings for the source data should be correct

Enter a **Chart title** of **Comparative sales (m) of top 10 albums by label** and press **Next**.

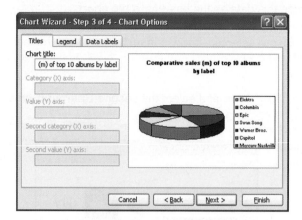

Figure 9.20: Giving the chart a title

 Click the top option to place the chart as a **new sheet**. You can give it a name, but this isn't important. Press **Finish** to create the new chart.

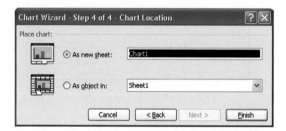

Figure 9.21: Inserting the pie chart as a new sheet

You should now have a pie chart that looks like Figure 9.22. You can switch between the **worksheet** and the **chart** by clicking on the tabs **Sheet1** and **Chart1** at the bottom of the embedded object.

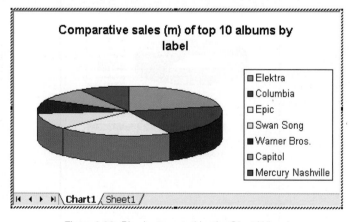

Figure 9.22: Pie chart created by the Chart Wizard

Click on a blank space in the document. This takes you out of editing mode for the chart and back to using Word. Click on the chart and click on the **Formatting** toolbar's **Center** button; this shifts the chart into the middle of the page.

Center

Since the totals for each label are calculated from data in the table, rather than explicitly listed, let's add them to the pie chart.

 Double-click the pie chart to go into edit mode. Select the chart area by clicking towards the edge of the embedded object, right-click and choose **Chart Options** as shown in Figure 9.23.

> **Syllabus Ref: AM3.4.4.3**
>
> Modify the formatting of a chart created from a table or pasted worksheet data.

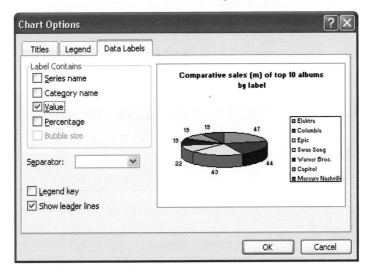

Figure 9.23: Editing options for an existing chart

Select the **Data Labels** tab and tick **Value** (see Figure 9.24). Then press **OK**.

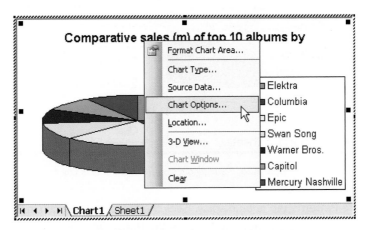

Figure 9.24: Adding value labels to the pie chart

You can also override the default formatting for any of the data points in the graph. Let's make the pie chart segment for Elektra bright red so that it stands out.

 Click on the segment that corresponds to **Elektra** (the one labelled **47**). The first time you click, the whole series will be selected (you will have an oval selection) – click again so that just the one segment is selected. Then **right-click** and select **Format Data Point**, as shown in Figure 9.25.

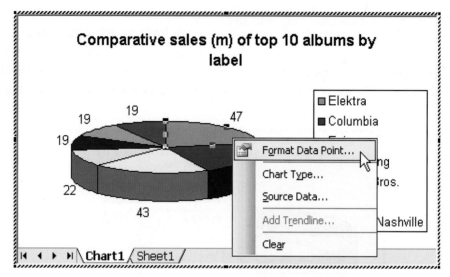

Figure 9.25: Formatting a single data point on a chart

 Make sure the **Patterns** tab is on display. Click the **red** colour swatch in the **Area** section to the right of the dialogue, as shown in Figure 9.26. Press **OK** to make the change.

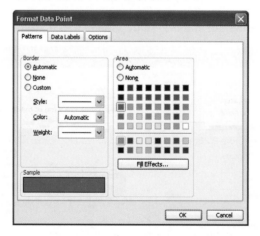

Figure 9.26: Changing the fill colour to red for a data point in a chart

Let's add a caption to further explain this second chart.

Click outside of the chart to stop editing it, then click once on the chart so that it becomes
selected. From the menu, select **Insert, Reference, Caption**. The **Caption** dialogue appears.

 Click the **Numbering** button to display the **Caption Numbering** dialogue. Set the format to
upper case letters and make sure **Include chapter number** is not ticked, as shown in
Figure 9.27. Press **OK**.

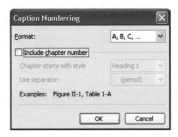

Figure 9.27: Changing the style of numbering for a caption

 The **Caption** dialogue should look like Figure 9.28, giving a **Caption** of **Figure A**. Press **OK** to
create the new caption.

Figure 9.28: Inserting a caption for an embedded worksheet

The new caption has been added, but does not have any descriptive text. The caption number is
simply a field (see page 88), so you can edit the text before and after it in the usual way.

 After the text **Figure A** in the new caption, type **: The sales figures of the top ten best-selling
albums of all time in the USA, in millions of units sold, grouped by record label.**

Insert a similar caption for the top chart, with the text **Graphical representation of Table 1**. Because this chart is free-floating, the caption will be created as a text box: you will need to drag this into position.

The final Music Sales document should look like Figure 9.29.

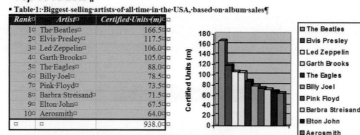

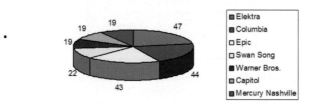

Figure 9.29: Final Music Sales document with two types of embedded chart

 Save **Music Sales.doc**.

Test yourself

1. In a new blank document, insert an **Excel worksheet** object and fill in the information about rivers given in Figure 9.30. Create a chart from this data (use the **Line – Column on 2 Axes** style from the **Custom Types** tab in the **Chart Wizard**). Change the page setup so that the **Orientation** is **Landscape** and change the image layout properties so that text flows to its left. Move and resize the chart, and add some text, so that your document looks like Figure 9.31. Notice the **wrapping break** symbol after the first paragraph – you can use **Insert, Break** to add one of these.

Wrapping Break

	A	B	C	D	E	F	G
1	River	Basin (x1000 sq. miles)	Length (miles)				
2	Amazon	2722	4000				
3	Nile	1107	3500				
4	Congo	1425	3000				
5	Yangtze	650	3000				
6	Volga	563	2300				
7							
8							
9							
10							

I◄ ◄ ► ►I \ Sheet1 /

Figure 9.30: Excel worksheet showing river data

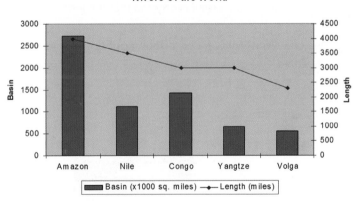

This·is·a·selection·of·some·rivers,·not·the·five·largest·ones.· The·chart·shows·their·lengths· and·the·areas·of·their·drainage· basins.

Now·we·will·go·on·to·look·at·some·of·the·world's·seas·and·oceans…¶

Figure 9.31: Chart of river data, with text wrapping around it

2. Experiment with adding some different types of object – for example the options available under **Insert, Diagram** – to a document.

10 Printing

Introduction

This chapter groups together some of the more advanced topics that are closely related to printing – such as adding **watermarks**, creating a **mail merge** and **printing specific pages** – which go beyond the simple 'Ctrl-P Print' technique. This chapter is also a convenient place to look at creating and using **macros**.

We will use the Master Brain invitation letter, the Music Sales document, the Timbleton Sailing Club handout and the recipe book that you have already created, to show how these advanced printing features work in practice.

In this chapter you will

 see how to add a draft **watermark** to your letter and how to remove it again

 record some **macros** that change the page setup for the music sales document, and add them to a toolbar

 see how to create a **mail merge** so that the letter can be personalised for each of its recipients

 see how Word's **advanced printing options** let you control exactly what part of a document is printed.

Watermarks

Traditionally, a **watermark** is a design pressed on to high-quality paper during its manufacture so that the brand name becomes visible when the paper is held up to the light. In word processing, the term **watermark** is extended to mean any light (typically grey) background picture or text added to a document.

Your first task is to add a **watermark** with the word **DRAFT** to the letter inviting past contestants to an anniversary Master Brain show. If you remove this watermark only when the letter is finished, it will make it less likely that you accidentally send out draft forms of the letter.

 Open the file **Master Brain.doc**.

 From the menu, select **Format, Background, Printed Watermark**. The **Printed Watermark** dialogue appears.

> **Syllabus Ref: AM3.4.5.7**
>
> Add a watermark to a document.

 Select the **Text watermark** option and choose **DRAFT** from the **Text** drop-down, as shown in Figure 10.1. Press **OK**.

Figure 10.1: Adding a watermark to a document

TIP

The **Text** drop-down is a **combo box**; this means you can either make a selection from the list or type in a different value.

Assuming you are in **Page Layout** view, you should now be able to see the word **DRAFT** in big grey letters running diagonally from the bottom-left to the top-right corner of the page. This **watermark** will come out on the printed copies too.

 Save and close the file.

Macros

A **macro** is a sequence of Word commands that have been recorded so that they can be played back later. If you find yourself having to repeat the same task over and over again, you will probably find that recording a macro will save you a lot of time.

If you often need to discuss draft documents in meetings, it can be useful to add line numbers and to create larger margins so that you have more room to make notes.

We are going to create a pair of macros: the first will change the page setup to use **landscape** orientation, add **line numbering** and add a wide right **margin**; the second macro will switch the page setup back again.

These macros will be saved inside the document **Music Sales.doc**, which you created in Chapters 6 and 9.

 Open the file **Music Sales.doc**.

> **Syllabus Ref: AM3.5.2.1**
>
> Record a simple macro.

 From the menu, select **Tools, Macro, Record New Macro**. The **Record Macro** dialogue will appear.

 Type **ReviewModeOn** as the **Macro name**. For **Store macro in**, select **Music Sales.doc (document)** from the drop-down list – normally you might want to store the macro as part of the standard template (**Normal.dot**) so that all documents could use it, but it is safer not to make global changes while you are learning how to do something. Add a suitable **Description**, as shown in Figure 10.2. Press **OK**.

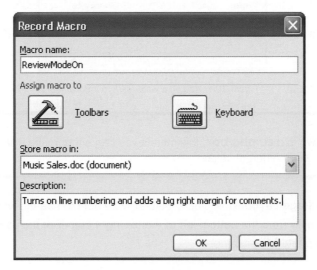

Figure 10.2: Recording a macro

You are now in **macro recording** mode; notice how your pointer has changed to show a cassette tape. All of the actions you perform from now until you stop recording will become part of your macro – if you make a mistake, it might be best to stop recording and then start again.

Macro
Recording

 From the menu, select **File**, **Page Setup**. The **Page Setup** dialogue appears. Switch to the **Layout** tab and press the **Line Numbers** button. Tick **Add line numbering**, as shown in Figure 10.3, and press **OK**.

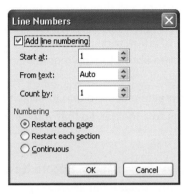

Figure 10.3: Adding line numbering

 Change to the **Margins** tab of the **Page Setup** dialogue. You want to shift the whole body of the document to the left, to create a wider right margin. Set the **Orientation** to **Landscape** and then reduce the **Left Margin** to **1.54 cm** and increase the **Right Margin** to **3.54 cm**, as shown in Figure 10.4. Press **OK** to apply the changes.

Type the new values for **1.54 cm** and **3.54 cm** instead of using the up and down arrows to the right of these fields, which can set values only to the nearest **0.1 cm**.

Figure 10.4: Changing to landscape orientation and increasing the right margin

You have now performed all of the commands for this macro, so you can tell Word to stop recording.

As soon as you started recording, the **Stop Recording** toolbar should have appeared. To stop recording, you can either press the **Stop** button (the square symbol on the left) on this toolbar or, from the menu, select **Tools**, **Macro**, **Stop Recording**.

You can use the other button to pause and then resume recording the macro.

 Use either of the methods given above to stop recording the macro.

Before using this new macro, let's create a second one to switch the page setup back to its original state. We will then add both macros to a toolbar, so that you can quickly toggle this 'reviewing mode' on and off.

 Start recording another macro (**Tools**, **Macro**, **Record New Macro**). Fill in the details shown in Figure 10.5 and then press **OK**. You are not allowed spaces in macro names (Word will let you type them, but will complain after you press **OK**), so it is a good idea to use a capital letter for the start of each word.

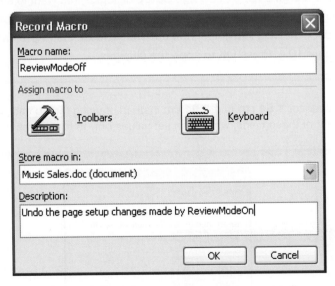

Figure 10.5: Recording a macro to turn 'review mode' off

 Record the actions necessary to undo the page setup changes you made before: select **File**, **Page Setup** and turn off the line numbering, change the page orientation back to **Portrait** and set the top and bottom margins back to **2.54 cm**.

 Stop recording the macro, using either of the techniques explained previously.

Soon we'll add these two macros to a toolbar, so that it is easy to toggle review mode on and off; first let's just try running the macros to check they work.

 From the menu, select **Tools, Macro, Macros.** Select **ReviewModeOn** and press **Run.**

Syllabus Ref: AM3.5.2.3
Run a macro.

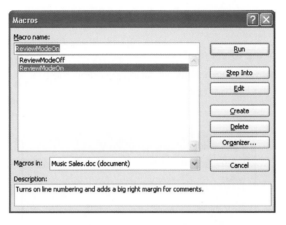

Figure 10.6: Running a macro

Word will prevent you from running unsigned macros if the **Macro Security** settings (**Tools, Options, Security**) are set too high.

The macro should automatically perform the page setup changes you made when you recorded it, so that your page becomes landscape with a wide right margin and the lines become numbered. Your screen should look something like Figure 10.7.

1 **Music·Sales¶**

2 **Top·10·Artists¶**

3 ▪ Table·1:·Biggest-selling·artists·of·all·time·in·the·USA,·based·on·album·sales¶

Rank	Artist	Certified·Units·(m)	
1	The·Beatles	166.5	
2	Elvis·Presley	117.5	
3	Led·Zeppelin	106.0	
4	Garth·Brooks	105.0	
5	The·Eagles	88.0	
6	Billy·Joel	78.5	
7	Pink·Floyd	73.5	
8	Barbra·Streisand	71.5	
9	Elton·John	67.5	
10	Aerosmith	64.0	
		938.0	

Figure·A:·Graphical·representation·of·Table·1¶

4 **Top·10·Albums¶**

5 ▪ Table·2:·Biggest-selling·albums·of·all·time·in·the·USA¶

Figure 10.7: Music Sales document after running the ReviewModeOn macro

 Use the same technique to run the **ReviewModeOff** macro. The document should change back to portrait orientation with equal left and right margins, and the line numbering should disappear.

This begins to demonstrate the advantage of macros: you can perform complicated tasks with just a few mouse clicks. For tasks that you need to perform very often, you can further reduce the time they take by adding the macros to a custom toolbar. Let's try this.

 Right-click on any of the toolbars at the top of Word. From the menu that is displayed, select the bottom option: **Customize**.

> **Syllabus Ref: AM3.5.2.4**
> Assign a macro to a custom button on a toolbar.

Figure 10.8: Customizing the toolbars

 Make sure that you are on the **Toolbars** tab. Press the **New** button. The **New Toolbar** dialogue is displayed. Type **ReviewModes** as the **Toolbar name**. Normally you would want to add the toolbar to a document template so that it was available to all documents created from that template, but it will be tidiest for this exercise to **Make toolbar available to** only **Music Sales.doc** (see Figure 10.9). Press **OK**.

Figure 10.9: Creating a new toolbar

The **Customize** dialogue should still be open. Switch to the **Commands** tab and select **Macros** from the **Categories** list. All of the available macros (including the two you have just recorded) should be listed under **Commands** on the right-hand side. Drag one of the new **ReviewMode** macros to the **ReviewMode** toolbar, as shown in Figure 10.10.

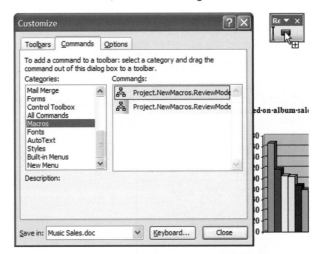

Figure 10.10: Dragging a macro command to the new toolbar

 Drag the other **ReviewMode** macro to the toolbar, which should then look like Figure 10.11.

Figure 10.11: ReviewModes toolbar with two text buttons

TIP

You can change the order of the two buttons by dragging them.

These text labels are a bit long-winded; let's change them and also add an icon for each button.

Right-click the **Project.NewMacros.ReviewModeOn** button. Click on **Name** in the menu that appears, reduce the name to **ReviewModeOn** (as shown in Figure 10.12) and then press the **Enter** key.

Figure 10.12: Renaming a toolbar button

Rename the other button **ReviewModeOff**.

It can be easier to find the right button to press if you add an image as well as text for your custom buttons.

 Right-click the **ReviewModeOn** button and from the menu select **Change Button Image**. Click on the image you would like to add to the button – since this button is used for reviewing, an eye seems appropriate (see Figure 10.13).

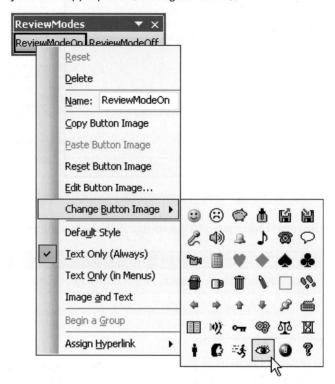

Figure 10.13: Changing the image on a toolbar button

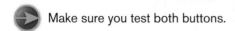 Add another suitable image for the **ReviewModeOff** button.

Figure 10.14: Custom macro toolbar with labels and images

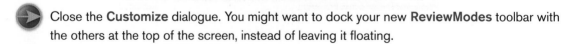 Close the **Customize** dialogue. You might want to dock your new **ReviewModes** toolbar with the others at the top of the screen, instead of leaving it floating.

Make sure you test both buttons.

Copying macros

Remember that you saved these macros in the **Music Sales.doc** document itself; this means that you can't easily run them in another document. This isn't a problem, though, since it's straightforward to copy macros between documents.

Let's try copying both of the macros to another of the documents you have created – **Timbleton Sailing Club.doc**.

> **Syllabus Ref: AM3.5.2.2**
>
> Copy a macro.

 From the menu select **Tools**, **Macro**, **Macros** and then press the **Organizer** button.

 In the **Organizer** dialogue (shown in Figure 10.15) switch to the **Macro Project Items** tab.

By default, Word expects you to be copying between the current open document and the **normal.dot** template. However, it does let you copy items directly between documents. Click on **Open File**.

 We want to change the right-hand file displayed in this dialogue from **Normal.dot** to **Timbleton Sailing Club.doc**. Press the right-hand **Close File** button. This clears the right-hand document and causes the **Close File** button to be renamed **Open File**.

 Change the **Files of type** filter from **Document Templates (*.dot)** to **Word Documents (*.doc)**, otherwise you won't be able to see the file! Navigate to the document **Timbleton Sailing Club.doc** and press **Open**.

 Back in the **Organizer** dialogue, select **NewMacros** in the left-hand list and press the **Copy** button. **NewMacros** should then appear in the list for transfer **To Timbleton Sailing Club.doc**.

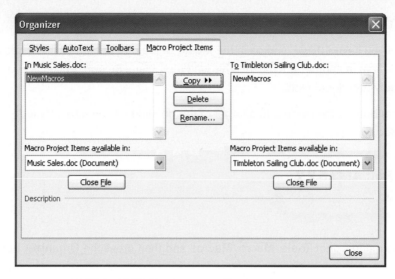

Figure 10.15: Copying macros between documents

 Press **Close**. You will be asked to confirm the background opening and saving of **Timbleton Sailing Club.doc** (so that the macros can be added): since this is exactly what you want, allow it.

 Save and close the file **Music Sales.doc**.

 Press **Open File**. Open **Timbleton Sailing Club.doc**; if you get a dialogue warning you that the document contains macros, just press **Enable**. Check that the document contains the two macros and that they work OK. You didn't copy the toolbar, so you'll have to run the macros via the **Tools** menu.

Mail merge

Now we'll carry on with the letter about the Master Brain anniversary show. In order to create customised versions of this letter to send to the contestants, we must use **mail merge**.

A **mail merge** takes a database of people's names and addresses and creates a letter for each person, personalised with their own details.

 Open the file **Master Brain.doc**.

Turning off the watermark

First, let's turn off the **draft** watermark that we added at the beginning of this chapter. Since we will be producing the final letters, we don't want them printed with the word **draft** running across them.

Turn off the **watermark** by going to **Format, Background, Printed Watermark** and selecting **No watermark**, as shown in Figure 10.16.

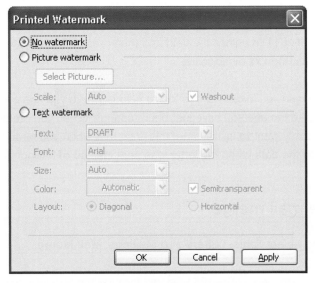

Figure 10.16: Removing the watermark

Locking and unlocking fields

Since mail merge works by changing the values of fields embedded in a template document, this is a convenient place to look at how you can lock fields against being changed.

The command for locking fields is unusual because there is no menu entry – you just have to remember the keyboard shortcut (**Ctrl+F11**). The same is true for unlocking fields (**Ctrl+Shift+F11**). Most actions in Word are easy to remember once you've done them a few times, but while locking and unlocking fields are easy actions to perform, you have no option but to learn the keys.

Syllabus Ref: AM3.3.3.3
Lock or unlock a field.

Of course, you could search for **lock field** in Word's **help** if you need a reminder!

 Click in the date field and type **xxx** anywhere in the middle of the date. Press **F9** to refresh the field. The date should return to its original form.

Another key worth remembering is **F9**, which refreshes the current field.

Place your insertion point in the date again (so it goes grey) and press **Ctrl+F11** to lock the field. Type **xxx** and press **F9** again. This time, because the field is locked, the **xxx** should remain.

Press **Ctrl+Shift+F11** to unlock the field and then press **F9** to refresh it. The date should be refreshed, so that the **xxx** disappears.

A useful situation in which you might want to lock a field is where you use a letter template with an automatic date field (like the one you have just been testing). When you create a letter and send it to someone, you probably want to fix the date; this is so that when you open the letter in the future, you will be able to see the date when the letter was sent instead of having it overwritten with the current date.

Setting up the mail merge

From the menu, select **Tools, Letters and Mailings, Mail Merge**.

The **Mail Merge** task pane opens. This will lead you through the six steps needed to create the customised letters.

Make sure the **document type** is set to **Letters** (see Figure 10.17) and then press **Next: Starting document**.

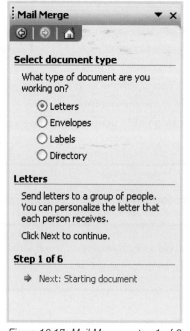

Figure 10.17: Mail Merge – step 1 of 6

For the **starting document** select **Use the current document** (Figure 10.18). Press **Next: Select recipients**.

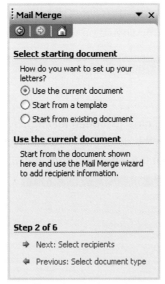

Figure 10.18: Mail Merge – step 2 of 6

Syllabus Ref: AM3.5.1.1

Edit a mail merge data source or data file.

We need to create a new list of recipients. Later in this chapter we'll see how to edit an existing list.

 In the **Select recipients** section, select **Type a new list**, then click the **Create** link.

Figure 10.19: Mail Merge – step 3 of 6

In the **New Address List** dialogue, click the **Customize** button. We won't need all of the default fields, so you can delete some by selecting them one by one in the list on the left and then pressing the **Delete** button: Delete the fields **Company Name**, **Country**, **Home Phone**, **Work Phone** and **E-mail Address**. You should be left with the fields shown in Figure 10.20. Press **OK**.

Figure 10.20: Deleting some of the default address fields

Enter the names and the addresses given in Figure 10.22 (see Figure 10.21). Press the **New Entry** button between addresses, but the **Close** button after the last one.

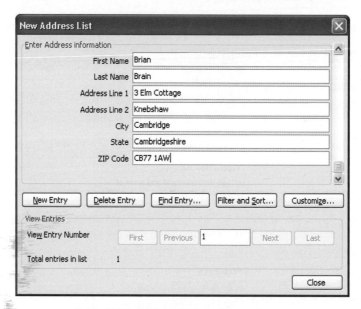

Figure 10.21: Adding addresses for a mail merge

Mr. Brian Brain	3 Elm Cottage	Knebshaw	Cambridge	Cambridgeshire	CB77 1AW
Ms. Sarah Brall	15 Cortex Close	Middleton	Cardiff	South Glamorgan	CF1 1BC
Gen. Keith Nolij	Fort Asmuch	Chilmslow	Reading	Berkshire	RG6 9AA
Mr. Richard Clever	The Laurels	Pootle	Ayr	Ayrshire	AY12 8SD
Mrs. Ira Member	1024 Long Road	West Dritton	Taunton	Somerset	TA3 9RT

Figure 10.22: Names and addresses of former Master Brain contestants

 After pressing **Close**, you will be asked where you want to save the database: save it as **Master Brain Contestants.mdb** in the same directory as your document.

The list of **Mail Merge Recipients** should look like Figure 10.23.

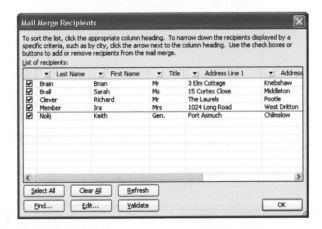

Figure 10.23: List of former contestants, ready for mail merge

Although there are only five people in this example, a real mail merge could have hundreds of recipients. Because of this, there are a couple of ways you can use this dialogue to manage the list of recipients: you can sort by any of the fields by clicking on its heading, or you can filter the records you want to use by clicking on the down arrows in the heading fields.

We'll only look at the first of these – sorting – but you might like to familiarise yourself with the filtering options too.

 TIP

If you had a large number of letters to send, you might use filtering so that you could send them in batches, for example surnames A–M and N–Z separately, or city by city.

 Click on the heading **Last Name**. The order of the records changes, so that they are sorted alphabetically by surname: Brain, Brall, Clever, Member, Nolij. This is the order that the letters will be created when you do the mail merge. Press **OK** to dismiss the **Mail Merge Recipients** dialogue.

> **Syllabus Ref: AM3.5.1.2**
> Sort data source or data file records.

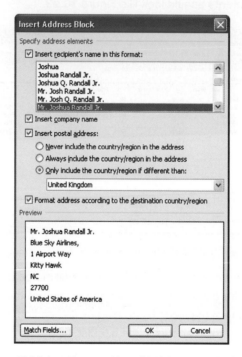

Back in the **Mail Merge** task pane, click **Next: Write your letter**.

Right-click on each of the comments in the document in turn and select **Delete Comment** for each.

Click on the text **[Click here and type recipients address]** and then press the **Delete** key.

Press the **Address Block** link in the **Mail Merge** task pane. The **Insert Address Block** dialogue appears, as shown in Figure 10.24. The default options will be fine, so just press **OK**. A field with the text **«AddressBlock»** appears in the document.

Figure 10.24: Inserting an address block in a mail merge letter

Select the line that says **Dear Sir or Madam:** (just below the date in the letter) and then press the **Delete** key. Click the **Greeting Line** link in the **Mail Merge** task pane.

The **Greeting Line** dialogue appears, as shown in Figure 10.25. Just accept the default selection by pressing **OK**.

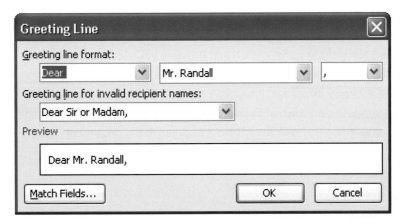

Figure 10.25: Adding a greeting line to a mail merge letter

 The text **«GreetingLine»** appears in the document. Press the **Enter** key if necessary so that the line **Master Brain will be ten years old** starts in a new paragraph.

«AddressBlock»¶
«GreetingLine»¶

Master· Brain· will· be· ten· year
anniversary· shows· where· prev
for·a·cash·prize·of·up·to·£500.¶

Figure 10.26: Section of document showing the two mail merge fields

 Click anywhere in the **«AddressBlock»** line and use the **Formatting** toolbar to change the paragraph style to **Inside Address** (make sure it isn't **Inside Address Name**). This is so there isn't a lot of space between the lines of the address when it is expanded from the database.

 Click anywhere in the **«GreetingLine»** line and change the paragraph style to **Attention Line**.

In the **Mail Merge** task pane, click **Next: Preview your letters**. The template letter will be automatically customised using the information from the first record in the mail merge database, as shown in Figure 10.27.

```
Mr·Brian·Brain¶
3·Elm·Cottage¶
Knebshaw¶
Cambridge¶
Cambridgeshire¶
CB77·1AW¶

Dear·Mr·Brain,¶

Master· Brain· will· be· ten· years· old· this· spring!· To· celebrate,· we· are· planning· several· special·
anniversary·shows·where·previous·contestants·can·again·pit·their·wits·against·the·Memory·Bank·for·
a·cash·prize·of·up·to·£500.¶
```

Figure 10.27: Part of a mail merge letter

 Click the double left and right arrows, as shown in Figure 10.28, to preview the letters that will be sent to the different recipients.

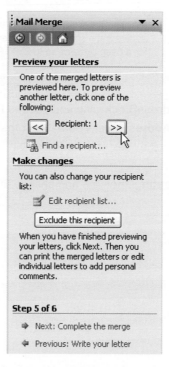

Figure 10.28: Switching between recipients while previewing mail merge letters

Click the link **Next: Complete the merge** to go to the next step.

Figure 10.29: Mail Merge – final step

 Rather than print all the letters now, we'll opt to create a new document that contains all of the letters, one per page. Press **Edit individual letters**. Make sure that the **Merge records** option is set to **All** (see Figure 10.30) and then press **OK**.

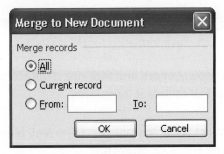

Figure 10.30: Selecting which records to use to complete the mail merge

Word creates a new document, each page of which is based on the template letter with the name and address details filled in from a single record in the mail merge database.

 Save the new document as **Mail Merge.doc** and close it. Also save and close the updated **Master Brain.doc**.

Syllabus Ref: AM3.5.1.1

Edit a mail merge data source or data file.

Edit a mail merge data source or data file

The process for editing a recipient list is very similar to the one we used to create the list originally. Let's go through the steps required to add, modify and delete a recipient.

 Open **Master Brain.doc**. The warning dialogue shown in Figure 10.31 should appear. Press the **Yes** button.

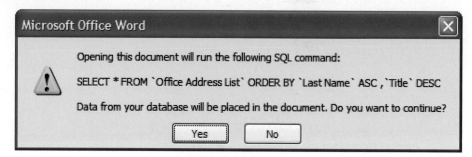

Figure 10.31: Warning about refreshing information from the database

Notice that the mail merge can refresh data from the database. This means that you could, if you preferred, maintain the contestant information using Microsoft Access, and only use Word for printing the letters.

The letter appears, populated with the information for Brian Brain. Let's update the list of recipients.

 From the menu, select **Tools, Letters and Mailings, Mail Merge**. The **Mail Merge** task pane appears, showing **Step 3 of 6: Select Recipients**.

 Click the **Edit recipient list** link in the task pane. The **Mail Merge Recipients** window appears, looking as it did in Figure 10.23 on page 183.

An alternative way to amend the list of recipients is by pressing the **Mail Merge Recipients** button on the **Mail Merge** toolbar.

 Select any of the names in the list and then press the **Edit** button. A window appears.

Adding a recipient

 Press the **New Entry** button and type in the information for Ivan Egghead, as shown in Figure 10.32. The bottom field is **EH99 1AX**.

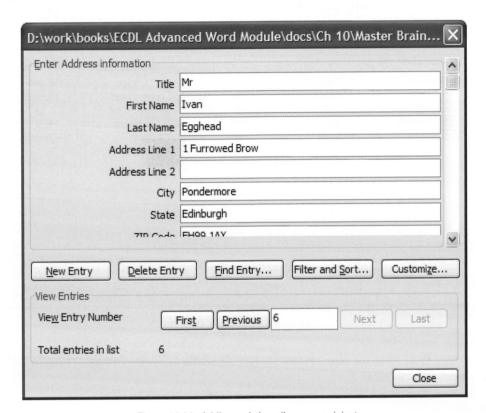

Figure 10.32: Adding a sixth mail merge recipient

Deleting a recipient

 Press the **Previous** button until the record for Richard Clever is displayed. Press the **Delete Entry** button, and press **Yes** on the confirmation dialogue.

Editing a recipient

 Press the **First** button to display the record for Brian Brain. Edit his address from **3** to **33 Elm Cottage**, then press the **Close** button.

The **Mail Merge Recipients** window should now look like Figure 10.33.

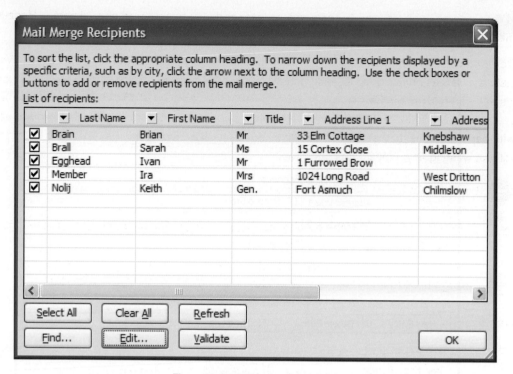

Figure 10.33: Edited list of recipients

 Press **OK** to close the **Mail Merge Recipients** window. Notice that Brian Brain's address is updated in the letter.

Click the **Next** link in the task pane twice to take you to **Step 5 of 6: Preview** your letters. Use the **double arrow** buttons to check that the three changes you have made (the addition, the deletion, and the edit) will be reflected in the letters produced by the mail merge.

Save and close **Master Brain.doc**.

Advanced printing options

In order to use the advanced printing options, we need a document with several pages. Because of this, we'll use the recipe book you started to create.

Don't worry if you don't have a printer – you can still work through this part of the exercise. Word 2003 installs a 'virtual' printer driver called **Microsoft Office Document Image Writer**, which you can use instead of a real printer. Rather than printing out on paper, this virtual printer driver writes out a file that you can then annotate, rearrange or email to other people. This feature is generally used for working with paper documents that are scanned in to Word, but it is also a handy way of trying out printing without wasting any paper.

 Load the document **Recipe Book.doc**.

 Switch to **Outline view** and expand the subdocuments. The recipe book should then have six pages (**i, ii, 1, 2, 3** and **4**).

 Change back to **Print Layout** view.

Let's try a simple print of the whole thing.

 From the menu, select **File, Print**. The **Print** dialogue will appear. From the drop-down list, select **Microsoft Office Document Image Writer**. Check that the other settings are as shown in Figure 10.34 and then press **OK**.

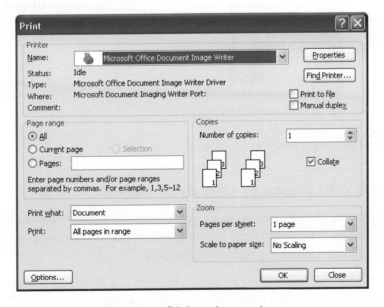

Figure 10.34: Printing a document image

Because we are printing to a file rather than on paper, Word will ask for the file name to save the document image as. Use the name **Recipe Book.mdi** and save it in the same folder as the recipe book itself. There is a tick box called **View Document Image** at the bottom of the dialogue – keep this ticked, so that the file is opened as soon as printing completes.

 The **Microsoft Office Document Imaging** tool opens, and loads the file **Recipe Book.mdi** that you have just saved. The window should look like Figure 10.35, showing that the print out has six pages.

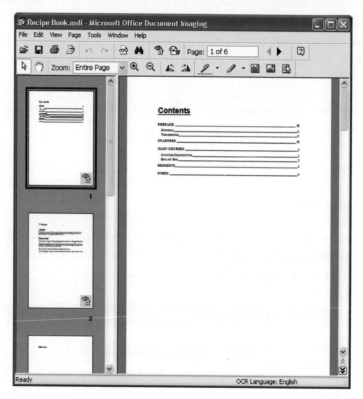

Figure 10.35: Viewing the image of a printed document

 Close the **Document Imaging** window.

Printing only odd pages or only even pages

Some printers give you the option of printing on both sides of the paper, and manage this automatically. However, often printers can only print on one side of the paper, so if you want to print on both sides then you need to turn the paper over manually.

Because all of the right-hand pages will be odd numbered (1, 3, 5) and all of the left-hand pages (which are the ones printed on the back of the right-hand pages) will be even (2, 4, 6), Word lets you print a document so that only the odd or only the even pages print. This means that you can print only the odd pages, turn the paper over and feed it back into the printer and then print only the even pages; you should then end up with all of the pages in the right order and printed double-sided.

Syllabus Ref: AM3.6.1.1
Print odd number pages only.

 Print the document again, but this time set the **Print** drop-down to **Odd pages**, as shown in Figure 10.36. Press **Print**. When asked, save the document as **Recipe Book Odd.mdi**.

Figure 10.36: Limiting printing to odd pages

When the document image loads, you will notice that it has only three pages – these are the pages that you would want on the right-hand side of your final book.

Syllabus Ref: AM3.6.1.2
Print even number pages only.

Printing only the even pages is done in exactly the same way; you just choose **Even pages** instead of **Odd pages** from the drop-down menu.

10 Printing

Printing only part of a document

Sometimes you just want to print part of a document – perhaps a specific paragraph or two, sometimes a particular range of pages. The **Print** dialogue makes this easy.

Let's try printing just the boiled egg recipe.

 Select the boiled egg recipe by clicking and dragging down its left-hand margin.

Syllabus Ref: AM3.6.1.3
Print a defined selection.

As before, select **File**, **Print** from the menu. This time change the **Page range** to **Selection**, as shown in Figure 10.37. Press **OK** to print.

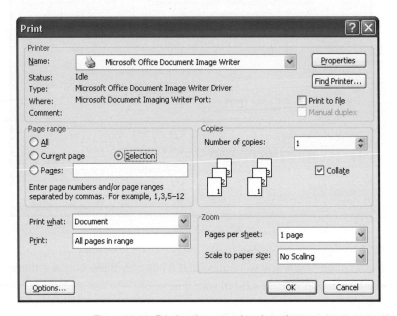

Figure 10.37: Printing the currently selected text

 Save the document image as **Recipe Book Selection.mdi**.

The result is a single-page print out containing just the boiled egg recipe.

You can also print a range of pages.

Syllabus Ref: AM3.6.1.4
Print a defined number of pages per sheet.

 From the menu, select **File, Print**. This time for the **Page range**, select **Pages** and type a value
3-4. This tells Word to print the range of pages from **3** to **4** inclusive. Also, set the **Pages per
sheet** to **2 pages**, as shown in Figure 10.38 – if you were actually printing the document, this
option would save paper by shrinking the pages and rotating them so that you end up with two
pages side-by-side on each printed side of paper. Press **OK**.

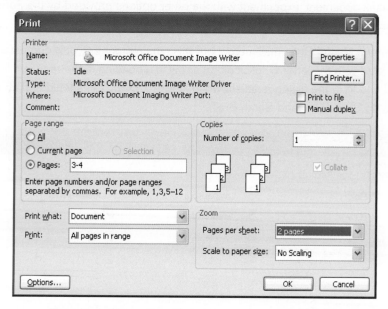

Figure 10.38: Printing a range of pages, with two pages per sheet

 TIP

If you wanted to print page 2, it would be slightly more complicated, because page
numbering restarts after the pages i and ii. You can tell Word which of the pages ii or
2 to print by specifying both the page number and the section number. For example,
p2s4 is page 2 in section 4, which resolves the ambiguity.

 Save the file as **Recipe Book Range.mdi**. The file should show the last two pages of the
original document, printed side-by-side.

Test yourself

1. It is a common typing error to get two letters the wrong way round. Again in **Music Sales.doc**, record a macro, called **Transpose**, that swaps the characters that are on the immediate left and right of the insertion point (tip: use the keyboard commands **Shift+Left, Ctrl+X, Right, Ctrl+V, Left**). Add this new macro to your custom toolbar. Don't forget to test it!

Figure 10.39: Custom toolbar showing the Transpose macro

2. You have seen how to add a simple text watermark to a document and how to remove it again. In a new blank document, experiment with the other options provided by the **Format, Background** menu.

3. Regenerate the Master Brain mail merge, but this time restrict it to only contestants living in cities that start with the letter **C** (click on an arrow in a heading in the recipient list, select **Advanced** and fill in the dialogue as shown in Figure 10.40). You should end up printing only two letters (to Brian Brain and Sarah Brall).

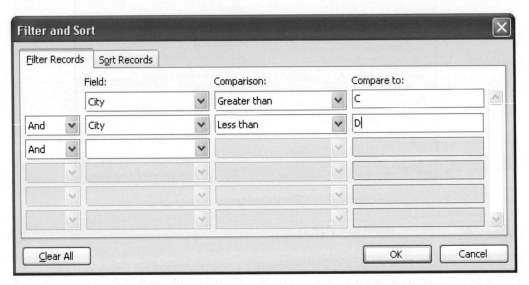

Figure 10.40: Restricting a mail merge to cities having names that start with C

TIP

The range between **C** and **D** is equivalent to all cities starting with the letter **C** (since **C** on its own comes before any longer words starting with **C** in a sorted list).

Index of Syllabus Topics

AM3.2.2 Table of Contents

AM3.2.3 Sections

AM3.2.4 Columns

AM3.3.1 Document Organisation

AM3.3.2 Referencing

AM3.3.3 Field Codes

AM3.3.4 Footnotes/Endnotes

AM3.3.5 Security

AM3.4.1 Tables

AM3.4.2 Forms

AM3.4.3 Text Boxes

AM3.4.4 Spreadsheets

Index